Daewoo Deluxe Air Fryer Cookbook UK

Amazingly Easy & Yummy Recipes to Fry, Grill, and Roast with Your Air Fryer

Kian Iqbal

Contents

SANDWICHES AND BURGERS RECIPES.................58

APPETIZERS AND SNACKS 68

VEGETARIANS RECIPES 78

VEGETABLE SIDE DISHES RECIPES.................89

INTRODUCTION

What is an Air Fryer?

What is an air fryer? This is a question many consumers are still asking. The name can be misleading, as this air cooker does much more than fry up diet-busting treats. It roasts, grills, fries, and even BAKES!

We're here to demystify the inner workings and results of this handy kitchen appliance.

Below, you'll learn how the air fryer uses convection currents to cook your foods, examine comparisons to similar kitchen products, discover amazing uses for this device, and more.

HOW DOES AN AIR FRYER WORK?

Air fryers simulate the traditional frying of foods by circulating hot air around food rather than submerging the food in oil. As with frying, properly prepared foods are crispy, juicy, golden brown, and flavorful.

Air fryers work due to the Maillard reaction, a scientific principle which refers to what we usually call "browning." A Maillard reaction occurs when the surface of a food item forms a crust due to dehydration, and the intense heat breaks down proteins, starches, and fibers. That is what gives fried, roasted, and baked foods their delicious, complex flavors.

An air fryer is a convection oven in miniature – a compact cylindrical countertop convection oven, to be exact (try saying that three times fast).

Basically, convection is the tendency of gases (or liquids) to move past each other when heated. Hot air rises, for example, simultaneously forcing cooler air to sink. Convection influences the weather; it is even at work in the molten rock that causes volcanic eruptions. But what, you may ask, does this have to do with your kitchen appliances?

Air fryers employ convection to rapidly and efficiently cook crisp foods. A heating element within the air fryer super-heats the air, producing natural convection currents. A fan within the appliance aids in air movement, circulating it even more rapidly. Perforations or holes in the cooking basket allow the hot air to flow freely around the food. This air movement increases heat transfer from the air to the food. Thus, your dinner gets done faster.

IS AIR FRIED FOOD HEALTHY?

Does an Air Fryer Use Radiation?

No. Unlike microwave ovens, which use a form of electromagnetic radiation called microwaves to excite water molecules, thus heating the food due to friction, air fryers do not use any form of radiation. Instead, air fryers employ a heating element similar to that found on any oven, toaster, or stovetop. The heating element works by converting an electrical current into heat.

Do Air Fryers Really Work?

We've already discussed how air fryers work. Now, you want to know, do they work, that is, do they work as shown on television commercials? Can they prepare crispy, amazing foods as advertised? Are air fryers worth the hype?

When used as designed and with quality recipes, air fryers do work. You can make crispy French fries, juicy roasted poultry, air fried veggies, and more. You may wish to consult our air fryer cooking charts to learn the best temperature at which to cook your favorite foods, and for how long.

WHAT IS THE BENEFIT OF AN AIR FRYER?

Consider the following reasons why an air fryer might be right for you:

Healthy Cooking

Everyone loves the taste of deep-fried foods, but many people must avoid these for health reasons. If you're looking to lower cholesterol or lose weight, your doctor may thank you for using an air fryer. Air fryers use around 75 percent less oil than deep fryers, providing a healthy alternative without sacrificing flavor.

Speed of Cooking

The air fryer's small convection oven preheats and cooks more quickly than a conventional oven. You'll have tasty meals in haste, with less wait!

Green Cooking

Have you "gone green?" Cooking with an air fryer can help. Most air fryers are energy efficient, and shorter cook times translate to less overall power usage.

Simple and Easy

Air fryers utilize simple controls, typically two knobs for cook time and temperature, or an easy to read digital display. You simply toss the food in oil (if desired), place it in the basket, and the air fryer does the rest.

Clean Up Is a Breeze

The baskets and pans of most air fryers are dishwasher safe for easy cleanup. Also, the enclosed nature of the air fryer prevents the splatters and spills associated with deep frying and pan frying.

Safe

Lacking the large oil vats of traditional deep fryers, air fryers eliminate the risk of serious burns from spilled oil. Also, air fryers are designed so that the exterior does not become dangerously hot to the touch.

FREQUENTLY ASKED QUESTIONS

What Types of Oils Can I Use in An Air Fryer?

Your oil mister will work great with any oils that have a high smoke point. This means the oil will withstand high temperatures before burning.

Avocado oil has a high smoke point of 570 degrees and gives food exceptional flavor. Other good choices include light olive oil (468 degrees), refined coconut oil (450 degrees), and peanut oil (450 degrees). You'll find that Bertolli brand oil and grapeseed oils are reliable.

Do You Put Oil in an Air Fryer?
An air fryer can prepare foods that would normally go in a deep fryer. Spraying foods like fries or onion rings with oil allows the intense circulating heat of the machine to cook a crisp exterior and tender interior. Most recipes only call for about 1 tablespoon of oil, which is best applied with a mister.

Fatty foods, like bacon, won't need you to add any oil. Leaner meats, however, will need some oiling to keep them from sticking to the pan.

Is Airfryer better than oven?

Do Air Fryers Work Better Than an Oven?
While air fryers and convection ovens both employ the science of convection, they have distinct differences in function and design. Both appliances may reduce cooking times due to fan-circulated, heated air.

Countertop convection ovens are generally larger than air fryers. They are designed for larger batch cooking, while air fryers typically handle two to six servings at a time.

Air fryers are easier to clean due to dishwasher safe parts and are very versatile when used with accessories.

What Can You Cook With an Air Fryer?
- French fries, tater tots, onion rings, and homemade potato chips
- Baked potatoes
- Grilled cheese sandwiches
- Roasted vegetables
- Corn on the cob
- Single-serve pizza
- Empanadas
- Egg rolls, spring rolls, and crab rangoon
- Donut holes
- Chicken
- Hamburgers
- Bacon
- Fish
- Steak

Steak? Yes, you read that right. You can cook juicy, tender steaks in an air fryer. Pizza? Well, a whole frozen pizza won't fit, but you can reheat leftovers like a champ, or make your own small, single serving pizzas using pita or naan bread.

As you can see, the possibilities are almost endless. If you can cook it at home, you'll most likely be able to cook it in your air fryer.

BREAD AND BREAKFAST

Hush Puffins

 Servings: 20   **Cooking Time: 8 Mins.**

Ingredients:

- 1 C. buttermilk
- ¼ C. butter, melted
- 2 eggs
- 1½ C. all-purpose flour
- 1½ C. cornmeal
- ⅓ C. sugar
- 1 tsp. baking soda
- 1 tsp. salt
- 4 scallions, minced
- vegetable oil

Directions:

1. Combine the buttermilk, butter and eggs in a large mixing bowl. In a second bowl combine the flour, cornmeal, sugar, baking soda and salt. Add the dry ingredients to the wet ingredients, stirring just to combine. Stir in the minced scallions and refrigerate the batter for 30 minutes.
2. Shape the batter into 2-inch balls. Brush or spray the balls with oil.
3. Preheat the air fryer to 360°F.
4. Air-fry the hush puffins in two batches at 360°F for 8 minutes, turning them over after 6 Mins. of the cooking process.
5. Serve warm with butter.

Not-so-english Muffins

 **Servings: 4** **Cooking Time: 10 Mins.**

Ingredients:

- 2 strips turkey bacon, cut in half crosswise
- 2 whole-grain English muffins, split
- 1 C. fresh baby spinach, long stems removed
- ¼ ripe pear, peeled and thinly sliced
- 4 slices Provolone cheese

Directions:

1. Place bacon strips in air fryer basket and cook for 2minutes. Check and separate strips if necessary so they cook evenly. Cook for 4 more minutes, until crispy. Remove and drain on paper towels.

2. Place split muffin halves in air fryer basket and cook at 390°F for 2minutes, just until lightly browned.

3. Open air fryer and top each muffin with a quarter of the baby spinach, several pear slices, a strip of bacon, and a slice of cheese.

4. Cook at 360°F for 2minutes, until cheese completely melts.

Brown Sugar Grapefruit

Servings: 2   **Cooking Time: 4 Mins.**

Ingredients:

- 1 grapefruit
- 2 to 4 tsp. brown sugar

Directions:

1. Preheat the air fryer to 400°F.

2. While the air fryer is Preheating, cut the grapefruit in half horizontally (in other words not through the stem or blossom end of the grapefruit). Slice the bottom of the grapefruit to help it sit flat on the counter if necessary. Using a sharp paring knife (serrated is great), cut around the grapefruit between the flesh of the fruit and the peel. Then, cut each segment away from the membrane so that it is sitting freely in the fruit.

3. Sprinkle 1 to 2 tsp. of brown sugar on each half of the prepared grapefruit. Set up a rack in the air fryer basket (use an air fryer rack or make your own rack with some crumpled up aluminum foil). You don't have to use a rack, but doing so will get the grapefruit closer to the element so that the brown sugar can caramelize a little better. Transfer the grapefruit half to the rack in the air fryer basket. Depending on how big your grapefruit are and what size air fryer you have, you may need to do each half separately to make sure they sit flat.

4. Air-fry at 400°F for 4 minutes.

5. Remove and let it cool for just a minute before enjoying.

Broccoli Cornbread

 **Servings: 6** **Cooking Time: 18 Mins.**

Ingredients:

- 1 C. frozen chopped broccoli, thawed and drained
- ¼ C. cottage cheese
- 1 egg, beaten
- 2 tbsp. minced onion
- 2 tbsp. melted butter
- ½ C. flour
- ½ C. yellow cornmeal
- 1 tsp. baking powder
- ½ tsp. salt
- ¼ C. milk, plus 2 tablespoons
- cooking spray

Directions:

1. Place thawed broccoli in colander and press with a spoon to squeeze out excess moisture.

2. Stir together all ingredients in a large bowl.

3. Spray 6 x 6-inch baking pan with cooking spray.

4. Spread batter in pan and cook at 330°F for 18 Mins. or until cornbread is lightly browned and loaf starts to pull away from sides of pan.

Quesadillas

 Servings: 4   **Cooking Time: 12 Mins.**

Ingredients:

- 4 eggs
- 2 tbsp. skim milk
- salt and pepper
- oil for misting or cooking spray
- 4 flour tortillas
- 4 tbsp. salsa
- 2 oz. Cheddar cheese, grated
- ½ small avocado, peeled and thinly sliced

Directions:

1. Preheat air fryer to 270°F.
2. Beat together eggs, milk, salt, and pepper.
3. Spray a 6 x 6-inch air fryer baking pan lightly with cooking spray and add egg mixture.
4. Cook 9minutes, stirring every 1 to 2minutes, until eggs are scrambled to your liking. Remove and set aside.
5. Spray one side of each tortilla with oil or cooking spray. Flip over.
6. Divide eggs, salsa, cheese, and avocado among the tortillas, covering only half of each tortilla.
7. Fold each tortilla in half and press down lightly.
8. Place 2 tortillas in air fryer basket and cook at 390°F for 3minutes or until cheese melts and outside feels slightly crispy. Repeat with remaining two tortillas.
9. Cut each cooked tortilla into halves or thirds.

Sweet And Spicy Pumpkin Scones

 Servings: 8   **Cooking Time: 8 Mins.**

Ingredients:

- 2 C. all-purpose flour
- 3 tbsp. packed brown sugar
- ½ tsp. baking powder
- ¼ tsp. baking soda
- ½ tsp. kosher salt
- ½ tsp. ground cinnamon
- ¼ tsp. ground ginger
- ¼ tsp. ground cardamom
- 4 tbsp. cold unsalted butter
- ½ C. plus 2 tbsp. pumpkin puree, divided
- 4 tbsp. milk, divided
- 1 large egg
- 1 C. powdered sugar

Directions:

1. In a large bowl, mix together the flour, brown sugar, baking powder, baking soda, salt, cinnamon, ginger, and cardamom. Using a pastry blender or two knives, cut in the butter until coarse crumbles appear.
2. In a small bowl, whisk together ½ C. of the pumpkin puree, 2 tbsp. of the milk, and the egg until combined. Pour the wet ingredients into the dry ingredients; stir to combine.
3. Form the dough into a ball and place onto a floured service. Press the dough out or use a rolling pin to roll out the dough until ½ inch thick and in a circle. Cut the dough into 8 wedges.
4. Bake at 360°F for 8 to 10 Mins. or until completely cooked through. Cook in batches as needed.
5. In a medium bowl, whisk together the powdered sugar, the remaining 2 tbsp. of pumpkin puree, and the remaining 2 tbsp. of milk. When the pumpkin scones have cooled, drizzle the pumpkin glaze over the top before serving.

Soft Pretzels

 Servings: 12   **Cooking Time: 6 Mins.**

Ingredients:

- 2 tsp. yeast
- 1 C. water, warm
- 1 tsp. sugar
- 1 tsp. salt
- 2½ C. all-purpose flour
- 2 tbsp. butter, melted
- 1 C. boiling water
- 1 tbsp. baking soda
- coarse sea salt
- melted butter

Directions:

1. Combine the yeast and water in a small bowl. Combine the sugar, salt and flour in the bowl of a stand mixer. With the mixer running and using the dough hook, drizzle in the yeast mixture and melted butter and knead dough until smooth and elastic – about 10 minutes. Shape into a ball and let the dough rise for 1 hour.
2. Punch the dough down to release any air and decide what size pretzels you want to make.
3. a. To make large pretzels, divide the dough into 12 portions.
4. b. To make medium sized pretzels, divide the dough into 24 portions.
5. c. To make mini pretzel knots, divide the dough into 48 portions.
6. Roll each portion into a skinny rope using both hands on the counter and rolling from the center to the ends of the rope. Spin the rope into a pretzel shape (or tie the rope into a knot) and place the tied pretzels on a parchment lined baking sheet.
7. Preheat the air fryer to 350°F.
8. Combine the boiling water and baking soda in a shallow bowl and whisk to dissolve (this mixture will bubble, but it will settle down). Let the water cool so that you can put your hands in it. Working in batches, dip the pretzels (top side down) into the baking soda-water mixture and let them soak for 30 seconds to a minute. (This step is what gives pretzels their texture and helps them to brown faster.) Then, remove the pretzels carefully and return them (top side up) to the baking sheet. Sprinkle the coarse salt on the top.
9. Air-fry in batches for 3 Mins. per side. When the pretzels are finished, brush them generously with the melted butter and enjoy them warm with some spicy mustard.

Bacon, Broccoli And Swiss Cheese Bread Pudding

 Servings: 2   **Cooking Time: 48 Mins.**

Ingredients:

- ½ lb. thick cut bacon, cut into ¼-inch pieces
- 3 C. brioche bread or rolls, cut into ½-inch cubes
- 3 eggs
- 1 C. milk
- ½ tsp. salt
- freshly ground black pepper
- 1 C. frozen broccoli florets, thawed and chopped
- 1½ C. grated Swiss cheese

Directions:

1. Preheat the air fryer to 400°F.

2. Air-fry the bacon for 6 Mins. until crispy, shaking the basket a few times while it cooks to help it cook evenly. Remove the bacon and set it aside on a paper towel.

3. Air-fry the brioche bread cubes for 2 Mins. to dry and toast lightly. (If your brioche is a few days old and slightly stale, you can omit this step.)

4. Butter a 6- or 7-inch cake pan. Combine all the ingredients in a large bowl and toss well. Transfer the mixture to the buttered cake pan, cover with aluminum foil and refrigerate the bread pudding overnight, or for at least 8 hours.

5. Remove the casserole from the refrigerator an hour before you plan to cook, and let it sit on the countertop to come to room temperature.

6. Preheat the air fryer to 330°F. Transfer the covered cake pan, to the basket of the air fryer, lowering the dish into the basket using a sling made of aluminum foil (fold a piece of aluminum foil into a strip about 2-inches wide by 24-inches long). Fold the ends of the aluminum foil over the top of the dish before returning the basket to the air fryer. Air-fry for 20 minutes. Remove the foil and air-fry for an additional 20 minutes. If the top starts to brown a little too much before the custard has set, simply return the foil to the pan. The bread pudding has cooked through when a skewer inserted into the center comes out clean.

DESSERTS AND SWEETS

Giant Oatmeal–peanut Butter Cookie

 **Servings: 4**   **Cooking Time: 18 Mins.**

Ingredients:

- 1 C. Rolled oats (not quick-cooking or steel-cut oats)
- ½ C. All-purpose flour
- ½ tsp. Ground cinnamon
- ½ tsp. Baking soda
- ⅓ C. Packed light brown sugar
- ¼ C. Solid vegetable shortening
- 2 tbsp. Natural-style creamy peanut butter
- 3 tbsp. Granulated white sugar
- 2 tbsp. (or 1 small egg, well beaten) Pasteurized egg substitute, such as Egg Beaters
- ⅓ C. Roasted, salted peanuts, chopped
- Baking spray

Directions:

1. Preheat the air fryer to 350°F .
2. Stir the oats, flour, cinnamon, and baking soda in a bowl until well combined.
3. Using an electric hand mixer at medium speed, beat the brown sugar, shortening, peanut butter, granulated white sugar, and egg substitute or egg (as applicable) until smooth and creamy, about 3 minutes, scraping down the inside of the bowl occasionally.
4. Scrape down and remove the beaters. Fold in the flour mixture and peanuts with a rubber spatula just until all the flour is moistened and the peanut bits are evenly distributed in the dough.
5. For a small air fryer, coat the inside of a 6-inch round cake pan with baking spray. For a medium air fryer, coat the inside of a 7-inch round cake pan with baking spray. And for a large air fryer, coat the inside of an 8-inch round cake pan with baking spray. Scrape and gently press the dough into the prepared pan, spreading it into an even layer to the perimeter.
6. Set the pan in the basket and air-fry undisturbed for 18 minutes, or until well browned.
7. Transfer the pan to a wire rack and cool for 15 minutes. Loosen the cookie from the perimeter with a spatula, then invert the pan onto a cutting board and let the cookie come free. Remove the pan and reinvert the cookie onto the wire rack. Cool for 5 Mins. more before slicing into wedges to serve.

Giant Vegan Chocolate Chip Cookie

 **Servings: 4**   **Cooking Time: 16 Mins.**

Ingredients:

- ⅔ C. All-purpose flour
- 5 tbsp. Rolled oats (not quick-cooking or steel-cut oats)
- ¼ tsp. Baking soda
- ¼ tsp. Table salt
- 5 tbsp. Granulated white sugar
- ¼ C. Vegetable oil
- 2½ tbsp. Tahini (see here)
- 2½ tbsp. Maple syrup
- 2 tsp. Vanilla extract
- ⅔ C. Vegan semisweet or bittersweet chocolate chips
- Baking spray

Directions:

1. Preheat the air fryer to 325°F (or 330°F, if that's the closest setting).
2. Whisk the flour, oats, baking soda, and salt in a bowl until well combined.
3. Using an electric hand mixer at medium speed, beat the sugar, oil, tahini, maple syrup, and vanilla until rich and creamy, about 3 minutes, scraping down the inside of the bowl occasionally.
4. Scrape down and remove the beaters. Fold in the flour mixture and chocolate chips with a rubber spatula just until all the flour is moistened and the chocolate chips are even throughout the dough.
5. For a small air fryer, coat the inside of a 6-inch round cake pan with baking spray. For a medium air fryer, coat the inside of a 7-inch round cake pan with baking spray. And for a large air fryer, coat the inside of an 8-inch round cake pan with baking spray. Scrape and gently press the dough into the prepared pan, spreading it into an even layer to the perimeter.
6. Set the pan in the basket and air-fry undisturbed for 16 minutes, or until puffed, browned, and firm to the touch.
7. Transfer the pan to a wire rack and cool for 10 minutes. Loosen the cookie from the perimeter with a spatula, then invert the pan onto a cutting board and let the cookie come free. Remove the pan and reinvert the cookie onto the wire rack. Cool for 5 Mins. more before slicing into wedges to serve.

Keto Cheesecake Cups

 **Servings: 6**　　 **Cooking Time: 10 Mins.**

Ingredients:

- 8 oz. cream cheese
- ¼ C. plain whole-milk Greek yogurt
- 1 large egg
- 1 tsp. pure vanilla extract
- 3 tbsp. monk fruit sweetener
- ¼ tsp. salt
- ½ C. walnuts, roughly chopped

Directions:

1. Preheat the air fryer to 315°F.

2. In a large bowl, use a hand mixer to beat the cream cheese together with the yogurt, egg, vanilla, sweetener, and salt. When combined, fold in the chopped walnuts.

3. Set 6 silicone muffin liners inside an air-fryer-safe pan. Note: This is to allow for an easier time getting the cheesecake bites in and out. If you don't have a pan, you can place them directly in the air fryer basket.

4. Evenly fill the cupcake liners with cheesecake batter.

5. Carefully place the pan into the air fryer basket and cook for about 10 minutes, or until the tops are lightly browned and firm.

6. Carefully remove the pan when done and place in the refrigerator for 3 hours to firm up before serving.

Tortilla Fried Pies

 Servings: 12　　 **Cooking Time: 5 Mins.**

Ingredients:

- 12 small flour tortillas (4-inch diameter)
- ½ C. fig preserves
- ¼ C. sliced almonds
- 2 tbsp. shredded, unsweetened coconut
- oil for misting or cooking spray

Directions:

1. Wrap refrigerated tortillas in damp paper towels and heat in microwave 30 seconds to warm.
2. Working with one tortilla at a time, place 2 tsp. fig preserves, 1 tsp. sliced almonds, and ½ tsp. coconut in the center of each.
3. Moisten outer edges of tortilla all around.
4. Fold one side of tortilla over filling to make a half-moon shape and press down lightly on center. Using the tines of a fork, press down firmly on edges of tortilla to seal in filling.
5. Mist both sides with oil or cooking spray.
6. Place hand pies in air fryer basket close but not overlapping. It's fine to lean some against the sides and corners of the basket. You may need to cook in 2 batches.
7. Cook at 390°F for 5minutes or until lightly browned. Serve hot.
8. Refrigerate any leftover pies in a closed container. To serve later, toss them back in the air fryer basket and cook for 2 or 3minutes to reheat.

Sea-salted Caramel Cookie Cups

 Servings: 12   **Cooking Time: 12 Mins.**

Ingredients:

- ⅓ C. butter
- ¼ C. brown sugar
- 1 tsp. vanilla extract
- 1 large egg
- 1 C. all-purpose flour
- ½ C. old-fashioned oats
- ½ tsp. baking soda
- ¼ tsp. salt
- ⅓ C. sea-salted caramel chips

Directions:

1. Preheat the air fryer to 300°F.

2. In a large bowl, cream the butter with the brown sugar and vanilla. Whisk in the egg and set aside.

3. In a separate bowl, mix the flour, oats, baking soda, and salt. Then gently mix the dry ingredients into the wet. Fold in the caramel chips.

4. Divide the batter into 12 silicon muffin liners. Place the cookie C. into the air fryer basket and cook for 12 Mins. or until a toothpick inserted in the center comes out clean.

5. Remove and let cool 5 Mins. before serving.

Fried Pineapple Chunks

 **Servings: 3** **Cooking Time: 10 Mins.**

Ingredients:

- 3 tbsp. Cornstarch
- 1 Large egg white, beaten until foamy
- 1 C. (4 ounces) Ground vanilla wafer cookies (not low-fat cookies)
- ¼ tsp. Ground dried ginger
- 18 (about 2¼ cups) Fresh 1-inch chunks peeled and cored pineapple

Directions:

1. Preheat the air fryer to 400°F.

2. Put the cornstarch in a medium or large bowl. Put the beaten egg white in a small bowl. Pour the cookie crumbs and ground dried ginger into a large zip-closed plastic bag, shaking it a bit to combine them.

3. Dump the pineapple chunks into the bowl with the cornstarch. Toss and stir until well coated. Use your cleaned fingers or a large fork like a shovel to pick up a few pineapple chunks, shake off any excess cornstarch, and put them in the bowl with the egg white. Stir gently, then pick them up and let any excess egg white slip back into the rest. Put them in the bag with the crumb mixture. Repeat the cornstarch-then-egg process until all the pineapple chunks are in the bag. Seal the bag and shake gently, turning the bag this way and that, to coat the pieces well.

4. Set the coated pineapple chunks in the basket with as much air space between them as possible. Even a fraction of an inch will work, but they should not touch. Air-fry undisturbed for 10 minutes, or until golden brown and crisp.

5. Gently dump the contents of the basket onto a wire rack. Cool for at least 5 Mins. or up to 15 Mins. before serving.

Molten Chocolate Almond Cakes

 **Servings: 3**   **Cooking Time: 13 Mins.**

Ingredients:

- butter and flour for the ramekins
- 4 oz. bittersweet chocolate, chopped
- ½ C. (1 stick) unsalted butter
- 2 eggs
- 2 egg yolks
- ¼ C. sugar
- ½ tsp. pure vanilla extract, or almond extract
- 1 tbsp. all-purpose flour
- 3 tbsp. ground almonds
- 8 to 12 semisweet chocolate discs (or 4 chunks of chocolate)
- cocoa powder or powdered sugar, for dusting
- toasted almonds, coarsely chopped

Directions:

1. Butter and flour three (6-ounce) ramekins. (Butter the ramekins and then coat the butter with flour by shaking it around in the ramekin and dumping out any excess.)

2. Melt the chocolate and butter together, either in the microwave or in a double boiler. In a separate bowl, beat the eggs, egg yolks and sugar together until light and smooth. Add the vanilla extract. Whisk the chocolate mixture into the egg mixture. Stir in the flour and ground almonds.

3. Preheat the air fryer to 330°F.

4. Transfer the batter carefully to the buttered ramekins, filling halfway. Place two or three chocolate discs in the center of the batter and then fill the ramekins to ½-inch below the top with the remaining batter. Place the ramekins into the air fryer basket and air-fry at 330°F for 13 minutes. The sides of the cake should be set, but the centers should be slightly soft. Remove the ramekins from the air fryer and let the cakes sit for 5 minutes. (If you'd like the cake a little less molten, air-fry for 14 Mins. and let the cakes sit for 4 minutes.)

5. Run a butter knife around the edge of the ramekins and invert the cakes onto a plate. Lift the ramekin off the plate slowly and carefully so that the cake doesn't break. Dust with cocoa powder or powdered sugar and serve with a scoop of ice cream and some coarsely chopped toasted almonds.

Honey-roasted Mixed Nuts

 Servings: 8   **Cooking Time: 15 Mins.**

Ingredients:

- ½ C. raw, shelled pistachios
- ½ C. raw almonds
- 1 C. raw walnuts
- 2 tbsp. filtered water
- 2 tbsp. honey
- 1 tbsp. vegetable oil
- 2 tbsp. sugar
- ½ tsp. salt

Directions:

1. Preheat the air fryer to 300°F.
2. Lightly spray an air-fryer-safe pan with olive oil; then place the pistachios, almonds, and walnuts inside the pan and place the pan inside the air fryer basket.
3. Cook for 15 minutes, shaking the basket every 5 Mins. to rotate the nuts.
4. While the nuts are roasting, boil the water in a small pan and stir in the honey and oil. Continue to stir while cooking until the water begins to evaporate and a thick sauce is formed. Note: The sauce should stick to the back of a wooden spoon when mixed. Turn off the heat.
5. Remove the nuts from the air fryer (cooking should have just completed) and spoon the nuts into the stovetop pan. Use a spatula to coat the nuts with the honey syrup.
6. Line a baking sheet with parchment paper and spoon the nuts onto the sheet. Lightly sprinkle the sugar and salt over the nuts and let cool in the refrigerator for at least 2 hours.
7. When the honey and sugar have hardened, store the nuts in an airtight container in the refrigerator.

Maple Cinnamon Cheesecake

 **Servings: 4**   **Cooking Time: 12 Mins.**

Ingredients:

- 6 sheets of cinnamon graham crackers
- 2 tbsp. butter
- 8 oz. Neufchâtel cream cheese
- 3 tbsp. pure maple syrup
- 1 large egg
- ½ tsp. ground cinnamon
- ¼ tsp. salt

Directions:

1. Preheat the air fryer to 350°F.
2. Place the graham crackers in a food processor and process until crushed into a flour. Mix with the butter and press into a mini air-fryer-safe pan lined at the bottom with parchment paper. Place in the air fryer and cook for 4 minutes.
3. In a large bowl, place the cream cheese and maple syrup. Use a hand mixer or stand mixer and beat together until smooth. Add in the egg, cinnamon, and salt and mix on medium speed until combined.
4. Remove the graham cracker crust from the air fryer and pour the batter into the pan.
5. Place the pan back in the air fryer, adjusting the temperature to 315°F. Cook for 18 minutes. Carefully remove when cooking completes. The top should be lightly browned and firm.
6. Keep the cheesecake in the pan and place in the refrigerator for 3 or more hours to firm up before serving.

POULTRY RECIPES

Coconut Chicken With Apricot-ginger Sauce

 Servings: 4   **Cooking Time: 8 Mins.**

Ingredients:

- 1½ lb. boneless, skinless chicken tenders, cut in large chunks (about 1¼ inches)
- salt and pepper
- ½ C. cornstarch
- 2 eggs
- 1 tbsp. milk
- 3 C. shredded coconut (see below)
- oil for misting or cooking spray
- Apricot-Ginger Sauce
- ½ C. apricot preserves
- 2 tbsp. white vinegar
- ¼ tsp. ground ginger
- ¼ tsp. low-sodium soy sauce
- 2 tsp. white or yellow onion, grated or finely minced

Directions:

1. Mix all ingredients for the Apricot-Ginger Sauce well and let sit for flavors to blend while you cook the chicken.
2. Season chicken chunks with salt and pepper to taste.
3. Place cornstarch in a shallow dish.
4. In another shallow dish, beat together eggs and milk.
5. Place coconut in a third shallow dish. (If also using panko breadcrumbs, as suggested below, stir them to mix well.)
6. Spray air fryer basket with oil or cooking spray.
7. Dip each chicken chunk into cornstarch, shake off excess, and dip in egg mixture.
8. Shake off excess egg mixture and roll lightly in coconut or coconut mixture. Spray with oil.
9. Place coated chicken chunks in air fryer basket in a single layer, close together but without sides touching.
10. Cook at 360°F for 4minutes, stop, and turn chunks over.
11. Cook an additional 4 Mins. or until chicken is done inside and coating is crispy brown.
12. Repeat steps 9 through 11 to cook remaining chicken chunks.

Tandoori Chicken Legs

 Servings: 2   **Cooking Time: 30 Mins.**

Ingredients:

- 1 C. plain yogurt
- 2 cloves garlic, minced
- 1 tbsp. grated fresh ginger
- 2 tsp. paprika
- 2 tsp. ground coriander
- 1 tsp. ground turmeric
- 1 tsp. salt
- ¼ tsp. ground cayenne pepper
- juice of 1 lime
- 2 bone-in, skin-on chicken legs
- fresh cilantro leaves

Directions:

1. Make the marinade by combining the yogurt, garlic, ginger, spices and lime juice. Make slashes into the chicken legs to help the marinade penetrate the meat. Pour the marinade over the chicken legs, cover and let the chicken marinate for at least an hour or overnight in the refrigerator.
2. Preheat the air fryer to 380°F.
3. Transfer the chicken legs from the marinade to the air fryer basket, reserving any extra marinade. Air-fry for 15 minutes. Flip the chicken over and pour the remaining marinade over the top. Air-fry for another 15 minutes, watching to make sure it doesn't brown too much. If it does start to get too brown, you can loosely tent the chicken with aluminum foil, tucking the ends of the foil under the chicken to stop it from blowing around.
4. Serve over rice with some fresh cilantro on top.

Crispy Duck With Cherry Sauce

 **Servings: 2**   **Cooking Time: 33 Mins.**

Ingredients:

- 1 whole duck (up to 5 pounds), split in half, back and rib bones removed
- 1 tsp. olive oil
- salt and freshly ground black pepper
- Cherry Sauce:
- 1 tbsp. butter
- 1 shallot, minced
- ½ C. sherry
- ¾ C. cherry preserves 1 C. chicken stock
- 1 tsp. white wine vinegar
- 1 tsp. fresh thyme leaves
- salt and freshly ground black pepper

Directions:

1. Preheat the air fryer to 400°F.

2. Trim some of the fat from the duck. Rub olive oil on the duck and season with salt and pepper. Place the duck halves in the air fryer basket, breast side up and facing the center of the basket.

3. Air-fry the duck for 20 minutes. Turn the duck over and air-fry for another 6 minutes.

4. While duck is air-frying, make the cherry sauce. Melt the butter in a large sauté pan. Add the shallot and sauté until it is just starting to brown – about 2 to 3 minutes. Add the sherry and deglaze the pan by scraping up any brown bits from the bottom of the pan. Simmer the liquid for a few minutes, until it has reduced by half. Add the cherry preserves, chicken stock and white wine vinegar. Whisk well to combine all the ingredients. Simmer the sauce until it thickens and coats the back of a spoon – about 5 to 7 minutes. Season with salt and pepper and stir in the fresh thyme leaves.

5. When the air fryer timer goes off, spoon some cherry sauce over the duck and continue to air-fry at 400°F for 4 more minutes. Then, turn the duck halves back over so that the breast side is facing up. Spoon more cherry sauce over the top of the duck, covering the skin completely. Air-fry for 3 more Mins. and then remove the duck to a plate to rest for a few minutes.

6. Serve the duck in halves, or cut each piece in half again for a smaller serving. Spoon any additional sauce over the duck or serve it on the side.

Chicken Adobo

 **Servings: 6**   **Cooking Time: 12 Mins.**

Ingredients:

- 6 boneless chicken thighs
- ¼ C. soy sauce or tamari
- ½ C. rice wine vinegar
- 4 cloves garlic, minced
- ⅛ tsp. crushed red pepper flakes
- ½ tsp. black pepper

Directions:

1. Place the chicken thighs into a resealable plastic bag with the soy sauce or tamari, the rice wine vinegar, the garlic, and the crushed red pepper flakes. Seal the bag and let the chicken marinate at least 1 hour in the refrigerator.
2. Preheat the air fryer to 400°F.
3. Drain the chicken and pat dry with a paper towel. Season the chicken with black pepper and liberally spray with cooking spray.
4. Place the chicken in the air fryer basket and cook for 9 minutes, turn over at 9 Mins. and check for an internal temperature of 165°F, and cook another 3 minutes.

Peachy Chicken Chunks With Cherries

 **Servings: 4** **Cooking Time: 16 Mins.**

Ingredients:

- ⅓ C. peach preserves
- 1 tsp. ground rosemary
- ½ tsp. black pepper
- ½ tsp. salt
- ½ tsp. marjoram
- 1 tsp. light olive oil
- 1 lb. boneless chicken breasts, cut in 1½-inch chunks
- oil for misting or cooking spray
- 10-ounce package frozen unsweetened dark cherries, thawed and drained

Directions:

1. In a medium bowl, mix together peach preserves, rosemary, pepper, salt, marjoram, and olive oil.

2. Stir in chicken chunks and toss to coat well with the preserve mixture.

3. Spray air fryer basket with oil or cooking spray and lay chicken chunks in basket.

4. Cook at 390°F for 7minutes. Stir. Cook for 8 more Mins. or until chicken juices run clear.

5. When chicken has cooked through, scatter the cherries over and cook for additional minute to heat cherries.

Italian Roasted Chicken Thighs

 **Servings: 6** **Cooking Time: 14 Mins.**

Ingredients:

- 6 boneless chicken thighs
- ½ tsp. dried oregano
- ½ tsp. garlic powder
- ½ tsp. sea salt
- ½ tsp. black pepper
- ¼ tsp. crushed red pepper flakes

Directions:

1. Pat the chicken thighs with paper towel.
2. In a small bowl, mix the oregano, garlic powder, salt, pepper, and crushed red pepper flakes. Rub the spice mixture onto the chicken thighs.
3. Preheat the air fryer to 400°F.
4. Place the chicken thighs in the air fryer basket and spray with cooking spray. Cook for 10 minutes, turn over, and cook another 4 minutes. When cooking completes, the internal temperature should read 165°F.

Coconut Curry Chicken With Coconut Rice

 Servings: 4   **Cooking Time: 56 Mins.**

Ingredients:

- 1 (14-ounce) can coconut milk
- 2 tbsp. green or red curry paste
- zest and juice of one lime
- 1 clove garlic, minced
- 1 tbsp. grated fresh ginger
- 1 tsp. ground cumin
- 1 (3- to 4-pound) chicken, cut into 8 pieces
- vegetable or olive oil
- salt and freshly ground black pepper

- fresh cilantro leaves
- For the rice:
- 1 C. basmati or jasmine rice
- 1 C. water
- 1 C. coconut milk
- ½ tsp. salt
- freshly ground black pepper

Directions:

1. Make the marinade by combining the coconut milk, curry paste, lime zest and juice, garlic, ginger and cumin. Coat the chicken on all sides with the marinade and marinate the chicken for 1 hour to overnight in the refrigerator.

2. Preheat the air fryer to 380°F.

3. Brush the bottom of the air fryer basket with oil. Transfer the chicken thighs and drumsticks from the marinade to the air fryer basket, letting most of the marinade drip off. Season to taste with salt and freshly ground black pepper.

4. Air-fry the chicken drumsticks and thighs at 380°F for 12 minutes. Flip the chicken over and continue to air-fry for another 12 minutes. Set aside and air-fry the chicken breast pieces at 380°F for 15 minutes. Turn the chicken breast pieces over and air-fry for another 12 minutes. Return the chicken thighs and drumsticks to the air fryer and air-fry for an additional 5 minutes.

5. While the chicken is cooking, make the coconut rice. Rinse the rice kernels with water and drain well. Place the rice in a medium saucepan with a tight fitting lid, along with the water, coconut milk, salt and freshly ground black pepper. Bring the mixture to a boil and then cover, reduce the heat and let it cook gently for 20 Mins. without lifting the lid. When the time is up, lift the lid, fluff with a fork and set aside.

6. Remove the chicken from the air fryer and serve warm with the coconut rice and fresh cilantro scattered around.

Jerk Chicken Drumsticks

 Servings: 2　　　🕐 **Cooking Time: 20 Mins.**

Ingredients:

- 1 or 2 cloves garlic
- 1 inch of fresh ginger
- 2 serrano peppers, (with seeds if you like it spicy, seeds removed for less heat)
- 1 tsp. ground allspice
- 1 tsp. ground nutmeg
- 1 tsp. chili powder
- ½ tsp. dried thyme
- ½ tsp. ground cinnamon
- ½ tsp. paprika
- 1 tbsp. brown sugar
- 1 tsp. soy sauce
- 2 tbsp. vegetable oil
- 6 skinless chicken drumsticks

Directions:

1. Combine all the ingredients except the chicken in a small chopper or blender and blend to a paste. Make slashes into the meat of the chicken drumsticks and rub the spice blend all over the chicken (a pair of plastic gloves makes this really easy). Transfer the rubbed chicken to a non-reactive covered container and let the chicken marinate for at least 30 Mins. or overnight in the refrigerator.
2. Preheat the air fryer to 400°F.
3. Transfer the drumsticks to the air fryer basket. Air-fry for 10 minutes. Turn the drumsticks over and air-fry for another 10 minutes. Serve warm with some rice and vegetables or a green salad.

Chicken Wellington

 **Servings: 2**   **Cooking Time: 31 Mins.**

Ingredients:

- 2 (5-ounce) boneless, skinless chicken breasts
- ½ C. White Worcestershire sauce
- 3 tbsp. butter
- ½ C. finely diced onion (about ½ onion)
- 8 oz. button mushrooms, finely chopped
- ¼ C. chicken stock
- 2 tbsp. White Worcestershire sauce (or white wine)

- salt and freshly ground black pepper
- 1 tbsp. chopped fresh tarragon
- 2 sheets puff pastry, thawed
- 1 egg, beaten
- vegetable oil

Directions:

1. Place the chicken breasts in a shallow dish. Pour the White Worcestershire sauce over the chicken coating both sides and marinate for 30 minutes.

2. While the chicken is marinating, melt the butter in a large skillet over medium-high heat on the stovetop. Add the onion and sauté for a few minutes, until it starts to soften. Add the mushrooms and sauté for 5 Mins. until the vegetables are brown and soft. Deglaze the skillet with the chicken stock, scraping up any bits from the bottom of the pan. Add the White Worcestershire sauce and simmer for 3 Mins. until the mixture reduces and starts to thicken. Season with salt and freshly ground black pepper. Remove the mushroom mixture from the heat and stir in the fresh tarragon. Let the mushroom mixture cool.

3. Preheat the air fryer to 360°F.

4. Remove the chicken from the marinade and transfer it to the air fryer basket. Tuck the small end of the chicken breast under the thicker part to shape it into a circle rather than an oval. Pour the marinade over the chicken and air-fry for 10 minutes.

5. Roll out the puff pastry and cut out two 6-inch squares. Brush the perimeter of each square with the egg wash. Place half of the mushroom mixture in the center of each puff pastry square. Place the chicken breasts, top side down on the mushroom mixture. Starting with one corner of puff pastry and working in one direction, pull the pastry up over the chicken to enclose it and press the ends of the pastry together in the middle. Brush the pastry with the egg wash to seal the edges. Turn the Wellingtons over and set aside.

6. To make a decorative design with the remaining puff pastry, cut out four 10-inch strips. For each Wellington, twist two of the strips together, place them over the chicken breast wrapped in puff pastry, and tuck the ends underneath to seal it. Brush the entire top and sides of the Wellingtons with the egg wash.

7. Preheat the air fryer to 350°F.

8. Spray or brush the air fryer basket with vegetable oil. Air-fry the chicken Wellingtons for 13 minutes. Carefully turn the Wellingtons over. Air-fry for another 8 minutes. Transfer to serving plates, light a candle and enjoy!

BEEF, PORK & LAMB RECIPES

Marinated Rib-eye Steak With Herb Roasted Mushrooms

 Servings: 2　　　 **Cooking Time: 10-15 Mins.**

Ingredients:

- 2 tbsp. Worcestershire sauce
- ¼ C. red wine
- 2 (8-ounce) boneless rib-eye steaks
- coarsely ground black pepper
- 8 oz. baby bella (cremini) mushrooms, stems trimmed and caps halved
- 2 tbsp. olive oil
- 1 tsp. dried parsley
- 1 tsp. fresh thyme leaves
- salt and freshly ground black pepper
- chopped fresh chives or parsley

Directions:

1. Combine the Worcestershire sauce and red wine in a shallow baking dish. Add the steaks to the marinade, pierce them several times with the tines of a fork or a meat tenderizer and season them generously with the coarsely ground black pepper. Flip the steaks over and pierce the other side in a similar fashion, seasoning again with the coarsely ground black pepper. Marinate the steaks for 2 hours.

2. Preheat the air fryer to 400°F.

3. Toss the mushrooms in a bowl with the olive oil, dried parsley, thyme, salt and freshly ground black pepper. Transfer the steaks from the marinade to the air fryer basket, season with salt and scatter the mushrooms on top.

4. Air-fry the steaks for 10 Mins. for medium-rare, 12 Mins. for medium, or 15 Mins. for well-done, flipping the steaks once halfway through the cooking time.

5. Serve the steaks and mushrooms together with the chives or parsley sprinkled on top. A good steak sauce or some horseradish would be a nice accompaniment.

Garlic And Oregano Lamb Chops

 **Servings: 4** **Cooking Time: 17 Mins.**

Ingredients:

- 1½ tbsp. Olive oil
- 1 tbsp. Minced garlic
- 1 tsp. Dried oregano
- 1 tsp. Finely minced orange zest
- ¾ tsp. Fennel seeds
- ¾ tsp. Table salt
- ¾ tsp. Ground black pepper
- 6 4-ounce, 1-inch-thick lamb loin chops

Directions:

1. Mix the olive oil, garlic, oregano, orange zest, fennel seeds, salt, and pepper in a large bowl. Add the chops and toss well to coat. Set aside as the air fryer heats, tossing one more time.
2. Preheat the air fryer to 400°F.
3. Set the chops bone side down in the basket (that is, so they stand up on their bony edge) with as much air space between them as possible. Air-fry undisturbed for 14 Mins. for medium-rare, or until an instant-read meat thermometer inserted into the thickest part of a chop (without touching bone) registers 132°F (not USDA-approved). Or air-fry undisturbed for 17 Mins. for well done, or until an instant-read meat thermometer registers 145°F (USDA-approved).
4. Use kitchen tongs to transfer the chops to a wire rack. Cool for 5 Mins. before serving.

Smokehouse-style Beef Ribs

Servings: 3   **Cooking Time: 25 Mins.**

Ingredients:

- ¼ tsp. Mild smoked paprika
- ¼ tsp. Garlic powder
- ¼ tsp. Onion powder
- ¼ tsp. Table salt
- ¼ tsp. Ground black pepper
- 3 10- to 12-ounce beef back ribs (not beef short ribs)

Directions:

1. Preheat the air fryer to 350°F .

2. Mix the smoked paprika, garlic powder, onion powder, salt, and pepper in a small bowl until uniform. Massage and pat this mixture onto the ribs.

3. When the machine is at temperature, set the ribs in the basket in one layer, turning them on their sides if necessary, sort of like they're spooning but with at least ¼ inch air space between them. Air-fry for 25 minutes, turning once, until deep brown and sizzling.

4. Use kitchen tongs to transfer the ribs to a wire rack. Cool for 5 Mins. before serving.

Sweet Potato–crusted Pork Rib Chops

 Servings: 2   **Cooking Time: 14 Mins.**

Ingredients:

- 2 Large egg white(s), well beaten
- 1½ C. (about 6 ounces) Crushed sweet potato chips (certified gluten-free, if a concern)
- 1 tsp. Ground cinnamon
- 1 tsp. Ground dried ginger
- 1 tsp. Table salt (optional)
- 2 10-ounce, 1-inch-thick bone-in pork rib chop(s)

Directions:

1. Preheat the air fryer to 375°F .
2. Set up and fill two shallow soup plates or small pie plates on your counter: one for the beaten egg white(s); and one for the crushed chips, mixed with the cinnamon, ginger, and salt (if using).
3. Dip a chop in the egg white(s), coating it on both sides as well as the edges. Let the excess egg white slip back into the rest, then set it in the crushed chip mixture. Turn it several times, pressing gently, until evenly coated on both sides and the edges. If necessary, set the chop aside and coat the remaining chop(s).
4. Set the chop(s) in the basket with as much air space between them as possible. Air-fry undisturbed for 12 minutes, or until crunchy and browned and an instant-read meat thermometer inserted into the center of a chop (without touching bone) registers 145°F. If the machine is at 360°F, you may need to add 2 Mins. to the cooking time.
5. Use kitchen tongs to transfer the chop(s) to a wire rack. Cool for 2 or 3 Mins. before serving.

Steak Fingers

 **Servings: 4** **Cooking Time: 8 Mins.**

Ingredients:

- 4 small beef cube steaks
- salt and pepper
- ½ C. flour
- oil for misting or cooking spray

Directions:

1. Cut cube steaks into 1-inch-wide strips.
2. Sprinkle lightly with salt and pepper to taste.
3. Roll in flour to coat all sides.
4. Spray air fryer basket with cooking spray or oil.
5. Place steak strips in air fryer basket in single layer, very close together but not touching. Spray top of steak strips with oil or cooking spray.
6. Cook at 390°F for 4minutes, turn strips over, and spray with oil or cooking spray.
7. Cook 4 more Mins. and test with fork for doneness. Steak fingers should be crispy outside with no red juices inside. If needed, cook an additional 4 Mins. or until well done. (Don't eat beef cube steak rare.)
8. Repeat steps 5 through 7 to cook remaining strips.

Pretzel-coated Pork Tenderloin

 **Servings: 4**   **Cooking Time: 10 Mins.**

Ingredients:

- 1 Large egg white(s)
- 2 tsp. Dijon mustard (gluten-free, if a concern)
- 1½ C. (about 6 ounces) Crushed pretzel crumbs (see the headnote; gluten-free, if a concern)
- 1 lb. (4 sections) Pork tenderloin, cut into ¼-pound (4-ounce) sections
- Vegetable oil spray

Directions:

1. Preheat the air fryer to 350°F .
2. Set up and fill two shallow soup plates or small pie plates on your counter: one for the egg white(s), whisked with the mustard until foamy; and one for the pretzel crumbs.
3. Dip a section of pork tenderloin in the egg white mixture and turn it to coat well, even on the ends. Let any excess egg white mixture slip back into the rest, then set the pork in the pretzel crumbs. Roll it several times, pressing gently, until the pork is evenly coated, even on the ends. Generously coat the pork section with vegetable oil spray, set it aside, and continue coating and spraying the remaining sections.
4. Set the pork sections in the basket with at least ¼ inch between them. Air-fry undisturbed for 10 minutes, or until an instant-read meat thermometer inserted into the center of one section registers 145°F.
5. Use kitchen tongs to transfer the pieces to a wire rack. Cool for 3 to 5 Mins. before serving.

Venison Backstrap

 **Servings: 4**   **Cooking Time: 10 Mins.**

Ingredients:

- 2 eggs
- ¼ C. milk
- 1 C. whole wheat flour
- ½ tsp. salt
- ¼ tsp. pepper
- 1 lb. venison backstrap, sliced
- salt and pepper
- oil for misting or cooking spray

Directions:

1. Beat together eggs and milk in a shallow dish.

2. In another shallow dish, combine the flour, salt, and pepper. Stir to mix well.

3. Sprinkle venison steaks with additional salt and pepper to taste. Dip in flour, egg wash, then in flour again, pressing in coating.

4. Spray steaks with oil or cooking spray on both sides.

5. Cooking in 2 batches, place steaks in the air fryer basket in a single layer. Cook at 360°F for 8minutes. Spray with oil, turn over, and spray other side. Cook for 2 Mins. longer, until coating is crispy brown and meat is done to your liking.

6. Repeat to cook remaining venison.

Pesto-rubbed Veal Chops

 **Servings: 2**   **Cooking Time: 12-15 Mins.**

Ingredients:

- ¼ C. Purchased pesto
- 2 10-ounce bone-in veal loin or rib chop(s)
- ½ tsp. Ground black pepper

Directions:

1. Preheat the air fryer to 400°F.

2. Rub the pesto onto both sides of the veal chop(s). Sprinkle one side of the chop(s) with the ground black pepper. Set aside at room temperature as the machine comes up to temperature.

3. Set the chop(s) in the basket. If you're cooking more than one chop, leave as much air space between them as possible. Air-fry undisturbed for 12 Mins. for medium-rare, or until an instant-read meat thermometer inserted into the center of a chop (without touching bone) registers 135°F (not USDA-approved). Or air-fry undisturbed for 15 Mins. for medium-well, or until an instant-read meat thermometer registers 145°F (USDA-approved).

4. Use kitchen tongs to transfer the chops to a cutting board or a wire rack. Cool for 5 Mins. before serving.

Natchitoches Meat Pies

 **Servings: 8** **Cooking Time: 12 Mins.**

Ingredients:

- Filling
- ½ lb. lean ground beef
- ¼ C. finely chopped onion
- ¼ C. finely chopped green bell pepper
- ⅛ tsp. salt
- ½ tsp. garlic powder
- ½ tsp. red pepper flakes
- 1 tbsp. low sodium Worcestershire sauce
- Crust

- 2 C. self-rising flour
- ¼ C. butter, finely diced
- 1 C. milk
- Egg Wash
- 1 egg
- 1 tbsp. water or milk
- oil for misting or cooking spray

Directions:

1. Mix all filling ingredients well and shape into 4 small patties.

2. Cook patties in air fryer basket at 390°F for 10 to 12minutes or until well done.

3. Place patties in large bowl and use fork and knife to crumble meat into very small pieces. Set aside.

4. To make the crust, use a pastry blender or fork to cut the butter into the flour until well mixed. Add milk and stir until dough stiffens.

5. Divide dough into 8 equal portions.

6. On a lightly floured surface, roll each portion of dough into a circle. The circle should be thin and about 5 inches in diameter, but don't worry about getting a perfect shape. Uneven circles result in a rustic look that many people prefer.

7. Spoon 2 tbsp. of meat filling onto each dough circle.

8. Brush egg wash all the way around the edge of dough circle, about ½-inch deep.

9. Fold each circle in half and press dough with tines of a dinner fork to seal the edges all the way around.

10. Brush tops of sealed meat pies with egg wash.

11. Cook filled pies in a single layer in air fryer basket at 360°F for 4minutes. Spray tops with oil or cooking spray, turn pies over, and spray bottoms with oil or cooking spray. Cook for an additional 2minutes.

12. Repeat previous step to cook remaining pies.

FISH AND SEAFOOD RECIPES

Salmon

Ingredients:

- Marinade
- 3 tbsp. low-sodium soy sauce
- 3 tbsp. rice vinegar
- 3 tbsp. ketchup
- 3 tbsp. olive oil
- 3 tbsp. brown sugar
- 1 tsp. garlic powder
- ½ tsp. ground ginger
- 4 salmon fillets (½-inch thick, 3 to 4 oz. each)
- cooking spray

Directions:

1. Mix all marinade ingredients until well blended.
2. Place salmon in sealable plastic bag or shallow container with lid. Pour marinade over fish and turn to coat well. Refrigerate for 30minutes.
3. Drain marinade, and spray air fryer basket with cooking spray.
4. Place salmon in basket, skin-side down.
5. Cook at 360°F for 10 minutes, watching closely to avoid overcooking. Salmon is done when just beginning to flake and still very moist.

Fish Sticks With Tartar Sauce

 **Servings: 2** **Cooking Time: 6 Mins.**

Ingredients:

- 12 oz. cod or flounder
- ½ C. flour
- ½ tsp. paprika
- 1 tsp. salt
- lots of freshly ground black pepper
- 2 eggs, lightly beaten
- 1½ C. panko breadcrumbs
- 1 tsp. salt
- vegetable oil
- Tartar Sauce:
- ¼ C. mayonnaise
- 2 tsp. lemon juice
- 2 tbsp. finely chopped sweet pickles
- salt and freshly ground black pepper

Directions:

1. Cut the fish into ¾-inch wide sticks or strips. Set up a dredging station. Combine the flour, paprika, salt and pepper in a shallow dish. Beat the eggs lightly in a second shallow dish. Finally, mix the breadcrumbs and salt in a third shallow dish. Coat the fish sticks by dipping the fish into the flour, then the egg and finally the breadcrumbs, coating on all sides in each step and pressing the crumbs firmly onto the fish. Place the finished sticks on a plate or baking sheet while you finish all the sticks.
2. Preheat the air fryer to 400°F.
3. Spray the fish sticks with the oil and spray or brush the bottom of the air fryer basket. Place the fish into the basket and air-fry at 400°F for 4 minutes, turn the fish sticks over, and air-fry for another 2 minutes.
4. While the fish is cooking, mix the tartar sauce ingredients together.
5. Serve the fish sticks warm with the tartar sauce and some French fries on the side.

Bacon-wrapped Scallops

 **Servings: 4**    **Cooking Time: 8 Mins.**

Ingredients:

- 16 large scallops
- 8 bacon strips
- ½ tsp. black pepper
- ¼ tsp. smoked paprika

Directions:

1. Pat the scallops dry with a paper towel. Slice each of the bacon strips in half. Wrap 1 bacon strip around 1 scallop and secure with a toothpick. Repeat with the remaining scallops. Season the scallops with pepper and paprika.

2. Preheat the air fryer to 350°F.

3. Place the bacon-wrapped scallops in the air fryer basket and cook for 4 minutes, shake the basket, cook another 3 minutes, shake the basket, and cook another 1 to 3 to minutes. When the bacon is crispy, the scallops should be cooked through and slightly firm, but not rubbery. Serve immediately.

Crispy Sweet-and-sour Cod Fillets

Servings: 3　　　**Cooking Time: 12 Mins.**

Ingredients:

- 1½ C. Plain panko bread crumbs (gluten-free, if a concern)
- 2 tbsp. Regular or low-fat mayonnaise (not fat-free; gluten-free, if a concern)
- ¼ C. Sweet pickle relish
- 3 4- to 5-ounce skinless cod fillets

Directions:

1. Preheat the air fryer to 400°F.
2. Pour the bread crumbs into a shallow soup plate or a small pie plate. Mix the mayonnaise and relish in a small bowl until well combined. Smear this mixture all over the cod fillets. Set them in the crumbs and turn until evenly coated on all sides, even on the ends.
3. Set the coated cod fillets in the basket with as much air space between them as possible. They should not touch. Air-fry undisturbed for 12 minutes, or until browned and crisp.
4. Use a nonstick-safe spatula to transfer the cod pieces to a wire rack. Cool for only a minute or two before serving hot.

Potato-wrapped Salmon Fillets

 **Servings: 3** **Cooking Time: 8 Mins.**

Ingredients:

- 1 Large 1-pound elongated yellow potato(es), peeled
- 3 6-ounce, 1½-inch-wide, quite thick skinless salmon fillets
- Olive oil spray
- ¼ tsp. Table salt
- ¼ tsp. Ground black pepper

Directions:

1. Preheat the air fryer to 400°F.
2. Use a vegetable peeler or mandoline to make long strips from the potato(es). You'll need anywhere from 8 to 12 strips per fillet, depending on the shape of the potato and of the salmon fillet.
3. Drape potato strips over a salmon fillet, overlapping the strips to create an even "crust." Tuck the potato strips under the fillet, overlapping the strips underneath to create as smooth a bottom as you can. Wrap the remaining fillet(s) in the same way.
4. Gently turn the fillets over. Generously coat the bottoms with olive oil spray. Turn them back seam side down and generously coat the tops with the oil spray. Sprinkle the salt and pepper over the wrapped fillets.
5. Use a nonstick-safe spatula to gently transfer the fillets seam side down to the basket. It helps to remove the basket from the machine and set it on your work surface (keeping in mind that the basket's hot). Leave as much air space as possible between the fillets. Air-fry undisturbed for 8 minutes, or until golden brown and crisp.
6. Use a nonstick-safe spatula to gently transfer the fillets to serving plates. Cool for a couple of Mins. before serving.

Fish And "chips"

Ingredients:

- ½ C. flour
- ½ tsp. paprika
- ¼ tsp. ground white pepper (or freshly ground black pepper)
- 1 egg
- ¼ C. mayonnaise
- 2 C. salt & vinegar kettle cooked potato chips, coarsely crushed
- 12 oz. cod
- tartar sauce
- lemon wedges

Directions:

1. Set up a dredging station. Combine the flour, paprika and pepper in a shallow dish. Combine the egg and mayonnaise in a second shallow dish. Place the crushed potato chips in a third shallow dish.

2. Cut the cod into 6 pieces. Dredge each piece of fish in the flour, then dip it into the egg mixture and then place it into the crushed potato chips. Make sure all sides of the fish are covered and pat the chips gently onto the fish so they stick well.

3. Preheat the air fryer to 370°F.

4. Place the coated fish fillets into the air fry basket. (It is ok if a couple of pieces slightly overlap or rest on top of other fillets in order to fit everything in the basket.)

5. Air-fry for 10 minutes, gently turning the fish over halfway through the cooking time.

6. Transfer the fish to a platter and serve with tartar sauce and lemon wedges.

Lobster Tails With Lemon Garlic Butter

 **Servings: 2**   **Cooking Time: 5 Mins.**

Ingredients:

- 4 oz. unsalted butter
- 1 tbsp. finely chopped lemon zest
- 1 clove garlic, thinly sliced
- 2 (6-ounce) lobster tails
- salt and freshly ground black pepper
- ½ C. white wine
- ½ lemon, sliced
- vegetable oil

Directions:

1. Start by making the lemon garlic butter. Combine the butter, lemon zest and garlic in a small saucepan. Melt and simmer the butter on the stovetop over the lowest possible heat while you prepare the lobster tails.

2. Prepare the lobster tails by cutting down the middle of the top of the shell. Crack the bottom shell by squeezing the sides of the lobster together so that you can access the lobster meat inside. Pull the lobster tail up out of the shell, but leave it attached at the base of the tail. Lay the lobster meat on top of the shell and season with salt and freshly ground black pepper. Pour a little of the lemon garlic butter on top of the lobster meat and transfer the lobster to the refrigerator so that the butter solidifies a little.

3. Pour the white wine into the air fryer drawer and add the lemon slices. Preheat the air fryer to 400°F for 5 minutes.

4. Transfer the lobster tails to the air fryer basket. Air-fry at 370° for 5 minutes, brushing more butter on halfway through cooking. (Add a minute or two if your lobster tail is more than 6-ounces.) Remove and serve with more butter for dipping or drizzling.

Salmon Puttanesca En Papillotte With Zucchini

 **Servings: 2** **Cooking Time: 17 Mins.**

Ingredients:

- 1 small zucchini, sliced into ¼-inch thick half moons
- 1 tsp. olive oil
- salt and freshly ground black pepper
- 2 (5-ounce) salmon fillets
- 1 beefsteak tomato, chopped (about 1 cup)
- 1 tbsp. capers, rinsed
- 10 black olives, pitted and sliced
- 2 tbsp. dry vermouth or white wine 2 tbsp. butter
- ¼ C. chopped fresh basil, chopped

Directions:

1. Preheat the air fryer to 400°F.

2. Toss the zucchini with the olive oil, salt and freshly ground black pepper. Transfer the zucchini into the air fryer basket and air-fry for 5 minutes, shaking the basket once or twice during the cooking process.

3. Cut out 2 large rectangles of parchment paper – about 13-inches by 15-inches each. Divide the air-fried zucchini between the two pieces of parchment paper, placing the vegetables in the center of each rectangle.

4. Place a fillet of salmon on each pile of zucchini. Season the fish very well with salt and pepper. Toss the tomato, capers, olives and vermouth (or white wine) together in a bowl. Divide the tomato mixture between the two fish packages, placing it on top of the fish fillets and pouring any juice out of the bowl onto the fish. Top each fillet with a tbsp. of butter.

5. Fold up each parchment square. Bring two edges together and fold them over a few times, leaving some space above the fish. Twist the open sides together and upwards so they can serve as handles for the packet, but don't let them extend beyond the top of the air fryer basket.

6. Place the two packages into the air fryer and air-fry at 400°F for 12 minutes. The packages should be puffed up and slightly browned when fully cooked. Once cooked, let the fish sit in the parchment for 2 minutes.

7. Serve the fish in the parchment paper, or if desired, remove the parchment paper before serving. Garnish with a little fresh basil.

Black Cod With Grapes, Fennel, Pecans And Kale

 **Servings: 2** **Cooking Time: 15 Mins.**

Ingredients:

- 2 (6- to 8-ounce) fillets of black cod (or sablefish)
- salt and freshly ground black pepper
- olive oil
- 1 C. grapes, halved
- 1 small bulb fennel, sliced ¼-inch thick
- ½ C. pecans
- 3 C. shredded kale
- 2 tsp. white balsamic vinegar or white wine vinegar
- 2 tbsp. extra virgin olive oil

Directions:

1. Preheat the air fryer to 400°F.
2. Season the cod fillets with salt and pepper and drizzle, brush or spray a little olive oil on top. Place the fish, presentation side up (skin side down), into the air fryer basket. Air-fry for 10 minutes.
3. When the fish has finished cooking, remove the fillets to a side plate and loosely tent with foil to rest.
4. Toss the grapes, fennel and pecans in a bowl with a drizzle of olive oil and season with salt and pepper. Add the grapes, fennel and pecans to the air fryer basket and air-fry for 5 Mins. at 400°F, shaking the basket once during the cooking time.
5. Transfer the grapes, fennel and pecans to a bowl with the kale. Dress the kale with the balsamic vinegar and olive oil, season to taste with salt and pepper and serve along side the cooked fish.

SANDWICHES AND BURGERS RECIPES

Philly Cheesesteak Sandwiches

 **Servings: 3**   **Cooking Time: 9 Mins.**

Ingredients:

- ¾ lb. Shaved beef
- 1 tbsp. Worcestershire sauce (gluten-free, if a concern)
- ¼ tsp. Garlic powder
- ¼ tsp. Mild paprika
- 6 tbsp. (1½ ounces) Frozen bell pepper strips (do not thaw)
- 2 slices, broken into rings Very thin yellow or white medium onion slice(s)
- 6 oz. (6 to 8 slices) Provolone cheese slices
- 3 Long soft rolls such as hero, hoagie, or Italian sub rolls, or hot dog buns (gluten-free, if a concern), split open lengthwise

Directions:

1. Preheat the air fryer to 400°F.
2. When the machine is at temperature, spread the shaved beef in the basket, leaving a ½-inch perimeter around the meat for good air flow. Sprinkle the meat with the Worcestershire sauce, paprika, and garlic powder. Spread the peppers and onions on top of the meat.
3. Air-fry undisturbed for 6 minutes, or until cooked through. Set the cheese on top of the meat. Continue air-frying undisturbed for 3 minutes, or until the cheese has melted.
4. Use kitchen tongs to divide the meat and cheese layers in the basket between the rolls or buns. Serve hot.

Eggplant Parmesan Subs

Servings: 2   **Cooking Time: 13 Mins.**

Ingredients:

- 4 Peeled eggplant slices (about ½ inch thick and 3 inches in diameter)
- Olive oil spray
- 2 tbsp. plus 2 tsp. Jarred pizza sauce, any variety except creamy
- ¼ C. (about ⅔ ounce) Finely grated Parmesan cheese
- 2 Small, long soft rolls, such as hero, hoagie, or Italian sub rolls (gluten-free, if a concern), split open lengthwise

Directions:

1. Preheat the air fryer to 350°F .

2. When the machine is at temperature, coat both sides of the eggplant slices with olive oil spray. Set them in the basket in one layer and air-fry undisturbed for 10 minutes, until lightly browned and softened.

3. Increase the machine's temperature to 375°F (or 370°F, if that's the closest setting—unless the machine is already at 360°F, in which case leave it alone). Top each eggplant slice with 2 tsp. pizza sauce, then 1 tbsp. cheese. Air-fry undisturbed for 2 minutes, or until the cheese has melted.

4. Use a nonstick-safe spatula, and perhaps a flatware fork for balance, to transfer the eggplant slices cheese side up to a cutting board. Set the roll(s) cut side down in the basket in one layer (working in batches as necessary) and air-fry undisturbed for 1 minute, to toast the rolls a bit and warm them up. Set 2 eggplant slices in each warm roll.

Perfect Burgers

 **Servings: 3** **Cooking Time: 13 Mins.**

Ingredients:

- 1 lb. 2 oz. 90% lean ground beef
- 1½ tbsp. Worcestershire sauce (gluten-free, if a concern)
- ½ tsp. Ground black pepper
- 3 Hamburger buns (gluten-free if a concern), split open

Directions:

1. Preheat the air fryer to 375°F .

2. Gently mix the ground beef, Worcestershire sauce, and pepper in a bowl until well combined but preserving as much of the meat's fibers as possible. Divide this mixture into two 5-inch patties for the small batch, three 5-inch patties for the medium, or four 5-inch patties for the large. Make a thumbprint indentation in the center of each patty, about halfway through the meat.

3. Set the patties in the basket in one layer with some space between them. Air-fry undisturbed for 10 minutes, or until an instant-read meat thermometer inserted into the center of a burger registers 160°F (a medium-well burger). You may need to add 2 Mins. cooking time if the air fryer is at 360°F.

4. Use a nonstick-safe spatula, and perhaps a flatware fork for balance, to transfer the burgers to a cutting board. Set the buns cut side down in the basket in one layer (working in batches as necessary) and air-fry undisturbed for 1 minute, to toast a bit and warm up. Serve the burgers in the warm buns.

Thanksgiving Turkey Sandwiches

 **Servings: 3** **Cooking Time: 10 Mins.**

Ingredients:

- 1½ C. Herb-seasoned stuffing mix (not cornbread-style; gluten-free, if a concern)
- 1 Large egg white(s)
- 2 tbsp. Water
- 3 5- to 6-ounce turkey breast cutlets
- Vegetable oil spray
- 4½ tbsp. Purchased cranberry sauce, preferably whole berry
- ⅛ tsp. Ground cinnamon
- ⅛ tsp. Ground dried ginger
- 4½ tbsp. Regular, low-fat, or fat-free mayonnaise (gluten-free, if a concern)
- 6 tbsp. Shredded Brussels sprouts
- 3 Kaiser rolls (gluten-free, if a concern), split open

Directions:

1. Preheat the air fryer to 375°F .

2. Put the stuffing mix in a heavy zip-closed bag, seal it, lay it flat on your counter, and roll a rolling pin over the bag to crush the stuffing mix to the consistency of rough sand. (Or you can pulse the stuffing mix to the desired consistency in a food processor.)

3. Set up and fill two shallow soup plates or small pie plates on your counter: one for the egg white(s), whisked with the water until foamy; and one for the ground stuffing mix.

4. Dip a cutlet in the egg white mixture, coating both sides and letting any excess egg white slip back into the rest. Set the cutlet in the ground stuffing mix and coat it evenly on both sides, pressing gently to coat well on both sides. Lightly coat the cutlet on both sides with vegetable oil spray, set it aside, and continue dipping and coating the remaining cutlets in the same way.

5. Set the cutlets in the basket and air-fry undisturbed for 10 minutes, or until crisp and brown. Use kitchen tongs to transfer the cutlets to a wire rack to cool for a few minutes.

6. Meanwhile, stir the cranberry sauce with the cinnamon and ginger in a small bowl. Mix the shredded Brussels sprouts and mayonnaise in a second bowl until the vegetable is evenly coated.

7. Build the sandwiches by spreading about 1½ tbsp. of the cranberry mixture on the cut side of the bottom half of each roll. Set a cutlet on top, then spread about 3 tbsp. of the Brussels sprouts mixture evenly over the cutlet. Set the other half of the roll on top and serve warm.

Chicken Club Sandwiches

 **Servings: 3** **Cooking Time: 15 Mins.**

Ingredients:

- 3 5- to 6-ounce boneless skinless chicken breasts
- 6 Thick-cut bacon strips (gluten-free, if a concern)
- 3 Long soft rolls, such as hero, hoagie, or Italian sub rolls (gluten-free, if a concern)
- 3 tbsp. Regular, low-fat, or fat-free mayonnaise (gluten-free, if a concern)
- 3 Lettuce leaves, preferably romaine or iceberg
- 6 ¼-inch-thick tomato slices

Directions:

1. Preheat the air fryer to 375°F .

2. Wrap each chicken breast with 2 strips of bacon, spiraling the bacon around the meat, slightly overlapping the strips on each revolution. Start the second strip of bacon farther down the breast but on a line with the start of the first strip so they both end at a lined-up point on the chicken breast.

3. When the machine is at temperature, set the wrapped breasts bacon-seam side down in the basket with space between them. Air-fry undisturbed for 12 minutes, until the bacon is browned, crisp, and cooked through and an instant-read meat thermometer inserted into the center of a breast registers 165°F. You may need to add 2 Mins. in the air fryer if the temperature is at 360°F.

4. Use kitchen tongs to transfer the breasts to a wire rack. Split the rolls open lengthwise and set them cut side down in the basket. Air-fry for 1 minute, or until warmed through.

5. Use kitchen tongs to transfer the rolls to a cutting board. Spread 1 tbsp. mayonnaise on the cut side of one half of each roll. Top with a chicken breast, lettuce leaf, and tomato slice. Serve warm.

Best-ever Roast Beef Sandwiches

 Servings: 6   **Cooking Time: 30-50 Mins.**

Ingredients:

- 2½ tsp. Olive oil
- 1½ tsp. Dried oregano
- 1½ tsp. Dried thyme
- 1½ tsp. Onion powder
- 1½ tsp. Table salt
- 1½ tsp. Ground black pepper
- 3 lb. Beef eye of round
- 6 Round soft rolls, such as Kaiser rolls or hamburger buns (gluten-free, if a concern), split open lengthwise
- ¾ C. Regular, low-fat, or fat-free mayonnaise (gluten-free, if a concern)
- 6 Romaine lettuce leaves, rinsed
- 6 Round tomato slices (¼ inch thick)

Directions:

1. Preheat the air fryer to 350°F .
2. Mix the oil, oregano, thyme, onion powder, salt, and pepper in a small bowl. Spread this mixture all over the eye of round.
3. When the machine is at temperature, set the beef in the basket and air-fry for 30 to 50 Mins. (the range depends on the size of the cut), turning the meat twice, until an instant-read meat thermometer inserted into the thickest piece of the meat registers 130°F for rare, 140°F for medium, or 150°F for well-done.
4. Use kitchen tongs to transfer the beef to a cutting board. Cool for 10 minutes. If serving now, carve into ⅛-inch-thick slices. Spread each roll with 2 tbsp. mayonnaise and divide the beef slices between the rolls. Top with a lettuce leaf and a tomato slice and serve. Or set the beef in a container, cover, and refrigerate for up to 3 days to make cold roast beef sandwiches anytime.

Thai-style Pork Sliders

Ingredients:

- 11 oz. Ground pork
- 2½ tbsp. Very thinly sliced scallions, white and green parts
- 4 tsp. Minced peeled fresh ginger
- 2½ tsp. Fish sauce (gluten-free, if a concern)
- 2 tsp. Thai curry paste (see the headnote; gluten-free, if a concern)
- 2 tsp. Light brown sugar
- ¾ tsp. Ground black pepper
- 4 Slider buns (gluten-free, if a concern)

Directions:

1. Preheat the air fryer to 375°F .

2. Gently mix the pork, scallions, ginger, fish sauce, curry paste, brown sugar, and black pepper in a bowl until well combined. With clean, wet hands, form about ⅓ C. of the pork mixture into a slider about 2½ inches in diameter. Repeat until you use up all the meat—3 sliders for the small batch, 4 for the medium, and 6 for the large. (Keep wetting your hands to help the patties adhere.)

3. When the machine is at temperature, set the sliders in the basket in one layer. Air-fry undisturbed for 14 minutes, or until the sliders are golden brown and caramelized at their edges and an instant-read meat thermometer inserted into the center of a slider registers 160°F.

4. Use a nonstick-safe spatula, and perhaps a flatware fork for balance, to transfer the sliders to a cutting board. Set the buns cut side down in the basket in one layer (working in batches as necessary) and air-fry undisturbed for 1 minute, to toast a bit and warm up. Serve the sliders warm in the buns.

Dijon Thyme Burgers

 **Servings: 3**   **Cooking Time: 18 Mins.**

Ingredients:

- 1 lb. lean ground beef
- ⅓ C. panko breadcrumbs
- ¼ C. finely chopped onion
- 3 tbsp. Dijon mustard
- 1 tbsp. chopped fresh thyme
- 4 tsp. Worcestershire sauce
- 1 tsp. salt
- freshly ground black pepper
- Topping (optional):
- 2 tbsp. Dijon mustard
- 1 tbsp. dark brown sugar
- 1 tsp. Worcestershire sauce
- 4 oz. sliced Swiss cheese, optional

Directions:

1. Combine all the burger ingredients together in a large bowl and mix well. Divide the meat into 4 equal portions and then form the burgers, being careful not to over-handle the meat. One good way to do this is to throw the meat back and forth from one hand to another, packing the meat each time you catch it. Flatten the balls into patties, making an indentation in the center of each patty with your thumb (this will help it stay flat as it cooks) and flattening the sides of the burgers so that they will fit nicely into the air fryer basket.

2. Preheat the air fryer to 370°F.

3. If you don't have room for all four burgers, air-fry two or three burgers at a time for 8 minutes. Flip the burgers over and air-fry for another 6 minutes.

4. While the burgers are cooking combine the Dijon mustard, dark brown sugar, and Worcestershire sauce in a small bowl and mix well. This optional topping to the burgers really adds a boost of flavor at the end. Spread the Dijon topping evenly on each burger. If you cooked the burgers in batches, return the first batch to the cooker at this time – it's ok to place the fourth burger on top of the others in the center of the basket. Air-fry the burgers for another 3 minutes.

5. Finally, if desired, top each burger with a slice of Swiss cheese. Lower the air fryer temperature to 330°F and air-fry for another minute to melt the cheese. Serve the burgers on toasted brioche buns, dressed the way you like them.

Crunchy Falafel Balls

 **Servings: 8** **Cooking Time: 16 Mins.**

Ingredients:

- 2½ C. Drained and rinsed canned chickpeas
- ¼ C. Olive oil
- 3 tbsp. All-purpose flour
- 1½ tsp. Dried oregano
- 1½ tsp. Dried sage leaves
- 1½ tsp. Dried thyme
- ¾ tsp. Table salt
- Olive oil spray

Directions:

1. Preheat the air fryer to 400°F.

2. Place the chickpeas, olive oil, flour, oregano, sage, thyme, and salt in a food processor. Cover and process into a paste, stopping the machine at least once to scrape down the inside of the canister.

3. Scrape down and remove the blade. Using clean, wet hands, form 2 tbsp. of the paste into a ball, then continue making 9 more balls for a small batch, 15 more for a medium one, and 19 more for a large batch. Generously coat the balls in olive oil spray.

4. Set the balls in the basket in one layer with a little space between them and air-fry undisturbed for 16 minutes, or until well browned and crisp.

5. Dump the contents of the basket onto a wire rack. Cool for 5 Mins. before serving.

APPETIZERS AND SNACKS

Sweet Potato Chips

Ingredients:

- 2 medium sweet potatoes, washed
- 2 C. filtered water
- 1 tbsp. avocado oil
- 2 tsp. brown sugar
- ½ tsp. salt

Directions:

1. Using a mandolin, slice the potatoes into ⅛-inch pieces.
2. Add the water to a large bowl. Place the potatoes in the bowl, and soak for at least 30 minutes.
3. Preheat the air fryer to 350°F.
4. Drain the water and pat the chips dry with a paper towel or kitchen cloth. Toss the chips with the avocado oil, brown sugar, and salt. Liberally spray the air fryer basket with olive oil mist.
5. Set the chips inside the air fryer, separating them so they're not on top of each other. Cook for 5 minutes, shake the basket, and cook another 5 minutes, or until browned.
6. Remove and let cool a few Mins. prior to serving. Repeat until all the chips are cooked.

Smoked Whitefish Spread

 **Servings: 1**   **Cooking Time: 10 Mins.**

Ingredients:

- ¾ lb. Boneless skinless white-flesh fish fillets, such as hake or trout
- 3 tbsp. Liquid smoke
- 3 tbsp. Regular, low-fat, or fat-free mayonnaise (gluten-free, if a concern)
- 2 tsp. Jarred prepared white horseradish (optional)
- ¼ tsp. Onion powder
- ¼ tsp. Celery seeds
- ¼ tsp. Table salt
- ¼ tsp. Ground black pepper

Directions:

1. Put the fish fillets in a zip-closed bag, add the liquid smoke, and seal closed. Rub the liquid smoke all over the fish , then refrigerate the sealed bag for 2 hours.
2. Preheat the air fryer to 400°F.
3. Set a 12-inch piece of aluminum foil on your work surface. Remove the fish fillets from the bag and set them in the center of this piece of foil (the fillets can overlap). Fold the long sides of the foil together and crimp them closed. Make a tight seam so no steam can escape. Fold up the ends and crimp to seal well.
4. Set the packet in the basket and air-fry undisturbed for 10 minutes.
5. Use kitchen tongs to transfer the foil packet to a wire rack. Cool for a minute or so. Open the packet, transfer the fish to a plate, and refrigerate for 30 minutes.
6. Put the cold fish in a food processor. Add the mayonnaise, horseradish (if using), onion powder, celery seeds, salt, and pepper. Cover and pulse to a slightly coarse spread, certainly not fully smooth.
7. For a more traditional texture, put the fish fillets in a bowl, add the other ingredients, and stir with a wooden spoon, mashing the fish with everything else to make a coarse paste.
8. Scrape the spread into a bowl and serve at once, or cover with plastic wrap and store in the fridge for up to 4 days.

Crabby Fries

Ingredients:

- 2 to 3 large russet potatoes, peeled and cut into ½-inch sticks
- 2 tbsp. vegetable oil
- 2 tbsp. butter
- 2 tbsp. flour
- 1 to 1½ C. milk
- ½ C. grated white Cheddar cheese
- pinch of nutmeg
- ½ tsp. salt
- freshly ground black pepper
- 1 tbsp. Old Bay® Seasoning

Directions:

1. Bring a large saucepan of salted water to a boil on the stovetop while you peel and cut the potatoes. Blanch the potatoes in the boiling salted water for 4 Mins. while you Preheat the air fryer to 400°F. Strain the potatoes and rinse them with cold water. Dry them well with a clean kitchen towel.

2. Toss the dried potato sticks gently with the oil and place them in the air fryer basket. Air-fry for 25 minutes, shaking the basket a few times while the fries cook to help them brown evenly.

3. While the fries are cooking, melt the butter in a medium saucepan. Whisk in the flour and cook for one minute. Slowly add 1 C. of milk, whisking constantly. Bring the mixture to a simmer and continue to whisk until it thickens. Remove the pan from the heat and stir in the Cheddar cheese. Add a pinch of nutmeg and season with salt and freshly ground black pepper. Transfer the warm cheese sauce to a serving dish. Thin with more milk if you want the sauce a little thinner.

4. As soon as the French fries have finished air-frying transfer them to a large bowl and season them with the Old Bay® Seasoning. Return the fries to the air fryer basket and air-fry for an additional 3 to 5 minutes. Serve immediately with the warm white Cheddar cheese sauce.

Kale Chips

 **Servings: 2**   **Cooking Time: 5 Mins.**

Ingredients:

- 4 Medium kale leaves, about 1 oz. each
- 2 tsp. Olive oil
- 2 tsp. Regular or low-sodium soy sauce or gluten-free tamari sauce

Directions:

1. Preheat the air fryer to 400°F.

2. Cut the stems from the leaves (all the stems, all the way up the leaf). Tear each leaf into three pieces. Put them in a large bowl.

3. Add the olive oil and soy or tamari sauce. Toss well to coat. You can even gently rub the leaves along the side of the bowl to get the liquids to stick to them.

4. When the machine is at temperature, put the leaf pieces in the basket in one layer. Air-fry for 5 minutes, turning and rearranging with kitchen tongs once halfway through, until the chips are dried out and crunchy. Watch carefully so they don't turn dark brown at the edges.

5. Gently pour the contents of the basket onto a wire rack. Cool for at least 5 Mins. before serving. The chips can keep for up to 8 hours uncovered on the rack (provided it's not a humid day).

Cheesy Tortellini Bites

 **Servings: 8**　　　 **Cooking Time: 10 Mins.**

Ingredients:

- 1 large egg
- ½ tsp. black pepper
- ½ tsp. garlic powder
- 1 tsp. Italian seasoning
- 12 oz. frozen cheese tortellini
- ½ C. panko breadcrumbs

Directions:

1. Preheat the air fryer to 380°F.
2. Spray the air fryer basket with an olive-oil-based spray.
3. In a medium bowl, whisk the egg with the pepper, garlic powder, and Italian seasoning.
4. Dip the tortellini in the egg batter and then coat with the breadcrumbs. Place each tortellini in the basket, trying not to overlap them. You may need to cook in batches to ensure the even crisp all around.
5. Bake for 5 minutes, shake the basket, and bake another 5 minutes.
6. Remove and let cool 5 minutes. Serve with marinara sauce, ranch, or your favorite dressing.

String Bean Fries

 Servings: 4 🕐 **Cooking Time: 6 Mins.**

Ingredients:

- ½ lb. fresh string beans
- 2 eggs
- 4 tsp. water
- ½ C. white flour
- ½ C. breadcrumbs
- ¼ tsp. salt
- ¼ tsp. ground black pepper
- ¼ tsp. dry mustard (optional)
- oil for misting or cooking spray

Directions:

1. Preheat air fryer to 360°F.
2. Trim stem ends from string beans, wash, and pat dry.
3. In a shallow dish, beat eggs and water together until well blended.
4. Place flour in a second shallow dish.
5. In a third shallow dish, stir together the breadcrumbs, salt, pepper, and dry mustard if using.
6. Dip each string bean in egg mixture, flour, egg mixture again, then breadcrumbs.
7. When you finish coating all the string beans, open air fryer and place them in basket.
8. Cook for 3minutes.
9. Stop and mist string beans with oil or cooking spray.
10. Cook for 3 moreminutes or until string beans are crispy and nicely browned.

Crispy Spiced Chickpeas

 **Servings: 2**   **Cooking Time: 20 Mins.**

Ingredients:

- 1 (15-ounce) can chickpeas, drained (or 1½ C. cooked chickpeas)
- ½ tsp. salt
- ½ tsp. chili powder
- ¼ tsp. ground cinnamon
- ⅛ tsp. smoked paprika
- pinch ground cayenne pepper
- 1 tbsp. olive oil

Directions:

1. Preheat the air fryer to 400°F.

2. Dry the chickpeas as well as you can with a clean kitchen towel, rubbing off any loose skins as necessary. Combine the spices in a small bowl. Toss the chickpeas with the olive oil and then add the spices and toss again.

3. Air-fry for 15 minutes, shaking the basket a couple of times while they cook.

4. Check the chickpeas to see if they are crispy enough and if necessary, air-fry for another 5 Mins. to crisp them further. Serve warm, or cool to room temperature and store in an airtight container for up to two weeks.

Crispy Wontons

 Servings: 8   **Cooking Time: 10 Mins.**

Ingredients:

- ½ C. refried beans
- 3 tbsp. salsa
- ¼ C. canned artichoke hearts, drained and patted dry
- ¼ C. frozen spinach, defrosted and squeezed dry
- 2 oz. cream cheese
- 1½ tsp. dried oregano, divided
- ¼ tsp. garlic powder
- ¼ tsp. onion powder
- ½ tsp. salt
- ¼ C. chopped pepperoni
- ¼ C. grated mozzarella cheese
- 1 tbsp. grated Parmesan
- 2 oz. cream cheese
- ½ tsp. dried oregano
- 32 wontons
- 1 C. water

Directions:

1. Preheat the air fryer to 370°F.
2. In a medium bowl, mix together the refried beans and salsa.
3. In a second medium bowl, mix together the artichoke hearts, spinach, cream cheese, oregano, garlic powder, onion powder, and salt.
4. In a third medium bowl, mix together the pepperoni, mozzarella cheese, Parmesan cheese, cream cheese, and the remaining ½ tsp. of oregano.
5. Get a towel lightly damp with water and ring it out. While working with the wontons, leave the unfilled wontons under the damp towel so they don't dry out.
6. Working with 8 wontons at a time, place 2 tsp. of one of the fillings into the center of the wonton, rotating among the different fillings (one filling per wonton). Working one at a time, use a pastry brush, dip the pastry brush into the water, and brush the edges of the dough with the water. Fold the dough in half to form a triangle and set aside. Continue until 8 wontons are formed. Spray the wontons with cooking spray and cover with a dry towel. Repeat until all 32 wontons have been filled.
7. Place the wontons into the air fryer basket, leaving space between the wontons, and cook for 5 minutes. Turn over and check for brownness, and then cook for another 5 minutes.

Sweet Chili Peanuts

 **Servings: 6**   **Cooking Time: 5 Mins.**

Ingredients:

- 2 C. (10 ounces) Shelled raw peanuts
- 2 tbsp. Granulated white sugar
- 2 tsp. Hot red pepper sauce, such as Cholula or Tabasco (gluten-free, if a concern)

Directions:

1. Preheat the air fryer to 400°F.

2. Toss the peanuts, sugar, and hot pepper sauce in a bowl until the peanuts are well coated.

3. When the machine is at temperature, pour the peanuts into the basket, spreading them into one layer as much as you can. Air-fry undisturbed for 3 minutes.

4. Shake the basket to rearrange the peanuts. Continue air-frying for 2 Mins. more, shaking and stirring the peanuts every 30 seconds, until golden brown.

5. Pour the peanuts onto a large lipped baking sheet. Spread them into one layer and cool for 5 Mins. before serving.

VEGETARIANS RECIPES

Broccoli Cheddar Stuffed Potatoes

 Servings: 2   **Cooking Time: 42 Mins.**

Ingredients:

- 2 large russet potatoes, scrubbed
- 1 tbsp. olive oil
- salt and freshly ground black pepper
- 2 tbsp. butter
- ¼ C. sour cream
- 3 tbsp. half-and-half (or milk)
- 1¼ C. grated Cheddar cheese, divided
- ¾ tsp. salt
- freshly ground black pepper
- 1 C. frozen baby broccoli florets, thawed and drained

Directions:

1. Preheat the air fryer to 400°F.

2. Rub the potatoes all over with olive oil and season generously with salt and freshly ground black pepper. Transfer the potatoes into the air fryer basket and air-fry for 30 minutes, turning the potatoes over halfway through the cooking process.

3. Remove the potatoes from the air fryer and let them rest for 5 minutes. Cut a large oval out of the top of both potatoes. Leaving half an inch of potato flesh around the edge of the potato, scoop the inside of the potato out and into a large bowl to prepare the potato filling. Mash the scooped potato filling with a fork and add the butter, sour cream, half-and-half, 1 C. of the grated Cheddar cheese, salt and pepper to taste. Mix well and then fold in the broccoli florets.

4. Stuff the hollowed out potato shells with the potato and broccoli mixture. Mound the filling high in the potatoes – you will have more filling than room in the potato shells.

5. Transfer the stuffed potatoes back to the air fryer basket and air-fry at 360°F for 10 minutes. Sprinkle the remaining Cheddar cheese on top of each stuffed potato, lower the heat to 330°F and air-fry for an additional minute or two to melt cheese.

Vegetable Couscous

 **Servings: 4**   **Cooking Time: 10 Mins.**

Ingredients:

- 4 oz. white mushrooms, sliced
- ½ medium green bell pepper, julienned
- 1 C. cubed zucchini
- ¼ small onion, slivered
- 1 stalk celery, thinly sliced
- ¼ tsp. ground coriander
- ¼ tsp. ground cumin
- salt and pepper
- 1 tbsp. olive oil
- Couscous
- ¾ C. uncooked couscous
- 1 C. vegetable broth or water
- ½ tsp. salt (omit if using salted broth)

Directions:

1. Combine all vegetables in large bowl. Sprinkle with coriander, cumin, and salt and pepper to taste. Stir well, add olive oil, and stir again to coat vegetables evenly.

2. Place vegetables in air fryer basket and cook at 390°F for 5minutes. Stir and cook for 5 more minutes, until tender.

3. While vegetables are cooking, prepare the couscous: Place broth or water and salt in large saucepan. Heat to boiling, stir in couscous, cover, and remove from heat.

4. Let couscous sit for 5minutes, stir in cooked vegetables, and serve hot.

Roasted Vegetable Lasagna

 **Servings: 6** **Cooking Time: 55 Mins.**

Ingredients:

- 1 zucchini, sliced
- 1 yellow squash, sliced
- 8 oz. mushrooms, sliced
- 1 red bell pepper, cut into 2-inch strips
- 1 tbsp. olive oil
- 2 C. ricotta cheese
- 2 C. grated mozzarella cheese, divided
- 1 egg
- 1 tsp. salt
- freshly ground black pepper
- ¼ C. shredded carrots

- ½ C. chopped fresh spinach
- 8 lasagna noodles, cooked
- Béchamel Sauce:
- 3 tbsp. butter
- 3 tbsp. flour
- 2½ C. milk
- ½ C. grated Parmesan cheese
- ½ tsp. salt
- freshly ground black pepper
- pinch of ground nutmeg

Directions:

1. Preheat the air fryer to 400°F.

2. Toss the zucchini, yellow squash, mushrooms and red pepper in a large bowl with the olive oil and season with salt and pepper. Air-fry for 10 minutes, shaking the basket once or twice while the vegetables cook.

3. While the vegetables are cooking, make the béchamel sauce and cheese filling. Melt the butter in a medium saucepan over medium-high heat on the stovetop. Add the flour and whisk, cooking for a couple of minutes. Add the milk and whisk vigorously until smooth. Bring the mixture to a boil and simmer until the sauce thickens. Stir in the Parmesan cheese and season with the salt, pepper and nutmeg. Set the sauce aside.

4. Combine the ricotta cheese, 1¼ C. of the mozzarella cheese, egg, salt and pepper in a large bowl and stir until combined. Fold in the carrots and spinach.

5. When the vegetables have finished cooking, build the lasagna. Use a baking dish that is 6 inches in diameter and 4 inches high. Cover the bottom of the baking dish with a little béchamel sauce. Top with two lasagna noodles, cut to fit the dish and overlapping each other a little. Spoon a third of the ricotta cheese mixture and then a third of the roasted veggies on top of the noodles. Pour ½ C. of béchamel sauce on top and then repeat these layers two more times: noodles – cheese mixture – vegetables – béchamel sauce. Sprinkle the remaining mozzarella cheese over the top. Cover the dish with aluminum foil, tenting it loosely so the aluminum doesn't touch the cheese.

6. Lower the dish into the air fryer basket using an aluminum foil sling (fold a piece of aluminum foil into a strip about 2-inches wide by 24-inches long). Fold the ends of the aluminum foil over the top of the dish before returning the basket to the air fryer. Air-fry for 45 minutes, removing the foil for the last 2 minutes, to slightly brown the cheese on top.

7. Let the lasagna rest for at least 20 Mins. to set up a little before slicing into it and serving.

Spaghetti Squash And Kale Fritters With Pomodoro Sauce

 Servings: 3 🕐 **Cooking Time: 45 Mins.**

Ingredients:

- 1½-pound spaghetti squash (about half a large or a whole small squash)
- olive oil
- ½ onion, diced
- ½ red bell pepper, diced
- 2 cloves garlic, minced
- 4 C. coarsely chopped kale
- salt and freshly ground black pepper
- 1 egg
- ⅓ C. breadcrumbs, divided
- ⅓ C. grated Parmesan cheese
- ½ tsp. dried rubbed sage
- pinch nutmeg
- Pomodoro Sauce:
- 2 tbsp. olive oil
- ½ onion, chopped
- 1 to 2 cloves garlic, minced
- 1 (28-ounce) can peeled tomatoes
- ¼ C. red wine
- 1 tsp. Italian seasoning
- 2 tbsp. chopped fresh basil, plus more for garnish
- salt and freshly ground black pepper
- ½ tsp. sugar (optional)

Directions:

1. Preheat the air fryer to 370°F.
2. Cut the spaghetti squash in half lengthwise and remove the seeds. Rub the inside of the squash with olive oil and season with salt and pepper. Place the squash, cut side up, into the air fryer basket and air-fry for 30 minutes, flipping the squash over halfway through the cooking process.
3. While the squash is cooking, Preheat a large sauté pan over medium heat on the stovetop. Add a little olive oil and sauté the onions for 3 minutes, until they start to soften. Add the red pepper and garlic and continue to sauté for an additional 4 minutes. Add the kale and season with salt and pepper. Cook for 2 more minutes, or

until the kale is soft. Transfer the mixture to a large bowl and let it cool.

4. While the squash continues to cook, make the Pomodoro sauce. Preheat the large sauté pan again over medium heat on the stovetop. Add the olive oil and sauté the onion and garlic for 2 to 3 minutes, until the onion begins to soften. Crush the canned tomatoes with your hands and add them to the pan along with the red wine and Italian seasoning and simmer for 20 minutes. Add the basil and season to taste with salt, pepper and sugar (if using).

5. When the spaghetti squash has finished cooking, use a fork to scrape the inside flesh of the squash onto a sheet pan. Spread the squash out and let it cool.

6. Once cool, add the spaghetti squash to the kale mixture, along with the egg, breadcrumbs, Parmesan cheese, sage, nutmeg, salt and freshly ground black pepper. Stir to combine well and then divide the mixture into 6 thick portions. You can shape the portions into patties, but I prefer to keep them a little random and unique in shape. Spray or brush the fritters with olive oil.

7. Preheat the air fryer to 370°F.

8. Brush the air fryer basket with a little olive oil and transfer the fritters to the basket. Air-fry the squash and kale fritters at 370°F for 15 minutes, flipping them over halfway through the cooking process.

9. Serve the fritters warm with the Pomodoro sauce spooned over the top or pooled on your plate. Garnish with the fresh basil leaves.

Lentil Fritters

 **Servings: 9** **Cooking Time: 12 Mins.**

Ingredients:

- 1 C. cooked red lentils
- 1 C. riced cauliflower
- ½ medium zucchini, shredded (about 1 cup)
- ¼ C. finely chopped onion
- ¼ tsp. salt
- ¼ tsp. black pepper
- ½ tsp. garlic powder
- ¼ tsp. paprika
- 1 large egg
- ⅓ C. quinoa flour

Directions:

1. Preheat the air fryer to 370°F.
2. In a large bowl, mix the lentils, cauliflower, zucchini, onion, salt, pepper, garlic powder, and paprika. Mix in the egg and flour until a thick dough forms.
3. Using a large spoon, form the dough into 9 large fritters.
4. Liberally spray the air fryer basket with olive oil. Place the fritters into the basket, leaving space around each fritter so you can flip them.
5. Cook for 6 minutes, flip, and cook another 6 minutes.
6. Remove from the air fryer and repeat with the remaining fritters. Serve warm with desired sauce and sides.

Basic Fried Tofu

 **Servings: 4**   **Cooking Time: 17 Mins.**

Ingredients:

- 14 oz. extra-firm tofu, drained and pressed
- 1 tbsp. sesame oil
- 2 tbsp. low-sodium soy sauce
- ¼ C. rice vinegar
- 1 tbsp. fresh grated ginger
- 1 clove garlic, minced
- 3 tbsp. cornstarch
- ¼ tsp. black pepper
- ⅛ tsp. salt

Directions:

1. Cut the tofu into 16 cubes. Set aside in a glass container with a lid.
2. In a medium bowl, mix the sesame oil, soy sauce, rice vinegar, ginger, and garlic. Pour over the tofu and secure the lid. Place in the refrigerator to marinate for an hour.
3. Preheat the air fryer to 350°F.
4. In a small bowl, mix the cornstarch, black pepper, and salt.
5. Transfer the tofu to a large bowl and discard the leftover marinade. Pour the cornstarch mixture over the tofu and toss until all the pieces are coated.
6. Liberally spray the air fryer basket with olive oil mist and set the tofu pieces inside. Allow space between the tofu so it can cook evenly. Cook in batches if necessary.
7. Cook 15 to 17 minutes, shaking the basket every 5 Mins. to allow the tofu to cook evenly on all sides. When it's done cooking, the tofu will be crisped and browned on all sides.
8. Remove the tofu from the air fryer basket and serve warm.

Egg Rolls

 **Servings: 4** **Cooking Time: 8 Mins.**

Ingredients:

- 🌀 1 clove garlic, minced
- 🌀 1 tsp. sesame oil
- 🌀 1 tsp. olive oil
- 🌀 ½ C. chopped celery
- 🌀 ½ C. grated carrots
- 🌀 2 green onions, chopped
- 🌀 2 oz. mushrooms, chopped
- 🌀 2 C. shredded Napa cabbage
- 🌀 1 tsp. low-sodium soy sauce
- 🌀 1 tsp. cornstarch
- 🌀 salt
- 🌀 1 egg
- 🌀 1 tbsp. water
- 🌀 4 egg roll wraps
- 🌀 olive oil for misting or cooking spray

Directions:

1. In a large skillet, sauté garlic in sesame and olive oils over medium heat for 1 minute.
2. Add celery, carrots, onions, and mushrooms to skillet. Cook 1 minute, stirring.
3. Stir in cabbage, cover, and cook for 1 minute or just until cabbage slightly wilts.
4. In a small bowl, mix soy sauce and cornstarch. Stir into vegetables to thicken. Remove from heat. Salt to taste if needed.
5. Beat together egg and water in a small bowl.
6. Divide filling into 4 portions and roll up in egg roll wraps. Brush all over with egg wash to seal.
7. Mist egg rolls very lightly with olive oil or cooking spray and place in air fryer basket.
8. Cook at 390°F for 4minutes. Turn over and cook 4 more minutes, until golden brown and crispy.

Stuffed Zucchini Boats

 Servings: 2   **Cooking Time: 20 Mins.**

Ingredients:

- olive oil
- ½ C. onion, finely chopped
- 1 clove garlic, finely minced
- ½ tsp. dried oregano
- ¼ tsp. dried thyme
- ¾ C. couscous
- 1½ C. chicken stock, divided
- 1 tomato, seeds removed and finely chopped
- ½ C. coarsely chopped Kalamata olives

- ½ C. grated Romano cheese
- ¼ C. pine nuts, toasted
- 1 tbsp. chopped fresh parsley
- 1 tsp. salt
- freshly ground black pepper
- 1 egg, beaten
- 1 C. grated mozzarella cheese, divided
- 2 thick zucchini

Directions:

1. Preheat a sauté pan on the stovetop over medium-high heat. Add the olive oil and sauté the onion until it just starts to soften–about 4 minutes. Stir in the garlic, dried oregano and thyme. Add the couscous and sauté for just a minute. Add 1¼ C. of the chicken stock and simmer over low heat for 3 to 5 minutes, until liquid has been absorbed and the couscous is soft. Remove the pan from heat and set it aside to cool slightly.

2. Fluff the couscous and add the tomato, Kalamata olives, Romano cheese, pine nuts, parsley, salt and pepper. Mix well. Add the remaining chicken stock, the egg and ½ C. of the mozzarella cheese. Stir to ensure everything is combined.

3. Cut each zucchini in half lengthwise. Then, trim each half of the zucchini into four 5-inch lengths. (Save the trimmed ends of the zucchini for another use.) Use a spoon to scoop out the center of the zucchini, leaving some flesh around the sides. Brush both sides of the zucchini with olive oil and season the cut side with salt and pepper.

4. Preheat the air fryer to 380°F.

5. Divide the couscous filling between the four zucchini boats. Use your hands to press the filling together and fill the inside of the zucchini. The filling should be mounded into the boats and rounded on top.

6. Transfer the zucchini boats to the air fryer basket and drizzle the stuffed zucchini boats with olive oil. Air-fry for 19 minutes. Then, sprinkle the remaining mozzarella cheese on top of the zucchini, pressing it down onto the filling lightly to prevent it from blowing around in the air fryer. Air-fry for one more minute to melt the cheese. Transfer the finished zucchini boats to a serving platter and garnish with the chopped parsley.

Veggie Fried Rice

 **Servings: 4** **Cooking Time: 25 Mins.**

Ingredients:

- 1 C. cooked brown rice
- ⅓ C. chopped onion
- ½ C. chopped carrots
- ½ C. chopped bell peppers
- ½ C. chopped broccoli florets
- 3 tbsp. low-sodium soy sauce
- 1 tbsp. sesame oil
- 1 tsp. ground ginger
- 1 tsp. ground garlic powder
- ½ tsp. black pepper
- ⅛ tsp. salt
- 2 large eggs

Directions:

1. Preheat the air fryer to 370°F.
2. In a large bowl, mix together the brown rice, onions, carrots, bell pepper, and broccoli.
3. In a small bowl, whisk together the soy sauce, sesame oil, ginger, garlic powder, pepper, salt, and eggs.
4. Pour the egg mixture into the rice and vegetable mixture and mix together.
5. Liberally spray a 7-inch springform pan (or compatible air fryer dish) with olive oil. Add the rice mixture to the pan and cover with aluminum foil.
6. Place a metal trivet into the air fryer basket and set the pan on top. Cook for 15 minutes. Carefully remove the pan from basket, discard the foil, and mix the rice. Return the rice to the air fryer basket, turning down the temperature to 350°F and cooking another 10 minutes.
7. Remove and let cool 5 minutes. Serve warm.

VEGETABLE SIDE DISHES RECIPES

Smashed Fried Baby Potatoes

 **Servings: 3** **Cooking Time: 18 Mins.**

Ingredients:

- 1½ lb. baby red or baby Yukon gold potatoes
- ¼ C. butter, melted
- 1 tsp. olive oil
- ½ tsp. paprika
- 1 tsp. dried parsley
- salt and freshly ground black pepper
- 2 scallions, finely chopped

Directions:

1. Bring a large pot of salted water to a boil. Add the potatoes and boil for 18 Mins. or until the potatoes are fork-tender.

2. Drain the potatoes and transfer them to a cutting board to cool slightly. Spray or brush the bottom of a drinking glass with a little oil. Smash or flatten the potatoes by pressing the glass down on each potato slowly. Try not to completely flatten the potato or smash it so hard that it breaks apart.

3. Combine the melted butter, olive oil, paprika, and parsley together.

4. Preheat the air fryer to 400°F.

5. Spray the bottom of the air fryer basket with oil and transfer one layer of the smashed potatoes into the basket. Brush with some of the butter mixture and season generously with salt and freshly ground black pepper.

6. Air-fry at 400°F for 10 minutes. Carefully flip the potatoes over and air-fry for an additional 8 Mins. until crispy and lightly browned.

7. Keep the potatoes warm in a 170°F oven or tent with aluminum foil while you cook the second batch. Sprinkle minced scallions over the potatoes and serve warm.

Latkes

 Servings: 12   **Cooking Time: 13 Mins.**

Ingredients:

- 1 russet potato
- ¼ onion
- 2 eggs, lightly beaten
- ⅓ C. flour
- ½ tsp. baking powder
- 1 tsp. salt
- freshly ground black pepper
- canola or vegetable oil, in a spray bottle
- chopped chives, for garnish
- apple sauce
- sour cream

Directions:

1. Shred the potato and onion with a coarse box grater or a food processor with the shredding blade. Place the shredded vegetables into a colander or mesh strainer and squeeze or press down firmly to remove the excess water.

2. Transfer the onion and potato to a large bowl and add the eggs, flour, baking powder, salt and black pepper. Mix to combine and then shape the mixture into patties, about ¼-cup of mixture each. Brush or spray both sides of the latkes with oil.

3. Preheat the air fryer to 400°F.

4. Air-fry the latkes in batches. Transfer one layer of the latkes to the air fryer basket and air-fry at 400°F for 12 to 13 minutes, flipping them over halfway through the cooking time. Transfer the finished latkes to a platter and cover with aluminum foil, or place them in a warm oven to keep warm.

5. Garnish the latkes with chopped chives and serve with sour cream and applesauce.

Rosemary Roasted Potatoes With Lemon

 **Servings: 4** **Cooking Time: 12 Mins.**

Ingredients:

- 1 lb. small red-skinned potatoes, halved or cut into bite-sized chunks
- 1 tbsp. olive oil
- 1 tsp. finely chopped fresh rosemary
- ¼ tsp. salt
- freshly ground black pepper
- 1 tbsp. lemon zest

Directions:

1. Preheat the air fryer to 400°F.
2. Toss the potatoes with the olive oil, rosemary, salt and freshly ground black pepper.
3. Air-fry for 12 Mins. (depending on the size of the chunks), tossing the potatoes a few times throughout the cooking process.
4. As soon as the potatoes are tender to a knifepoint, toss them with the lemon zest and more salt if desired.

Hawaiian Brown Rice

Servings: 4   **Cooking Time: 12 Mins.**

Ingredients:

- ¼ lb. ground sausage
- 1 tsp. butter
- ¼ C. minced onion
- ¼ C. minced bell pepper
- 2 C. cooked brown rice
- 1 8-ounce can crushed pineapple, drained

Directions:

1. Shape sausage into 3 or 4 thin patties. Cook at 390°F for 6 to 8minutes or until well done. Remove from air fryer, drain, and crumble. Set aside.

2. Place butter, onion, and bell pepper in baking pan. Cook at 390°F for 1 minute and stir. Cook 4 Mins. longer or just until vegetables are tender.

3. Add sausage, rice, and pineapple to vegetables and stir together.

4. Cook at 390°F for 2 minutes, until heated through.

Glazed Carrots

 **Servings: 4**   **Cooking Time: 10 Mins.**

Ingredients:

- ❀ 2 tsp. honey
- ❀ 1 tsp. orange juice
- ❀ ½ tsp. grated orange rind
- ❀ ⅛ tsp. ginger
- ❀ 1 lb. baby carrots
- ❀ 2 tsp. olive oil
- ❀ ¼ tsp. salt

Directions:

1. Combine honey, orange juice, grated rind, and ginger in a small bowl and set aside.

2. Toss the carrots, oil, and salt together to coat well and pour them into the air fryer basket.

3. Cook at 390°F for 5minutes. Shake basket to stir a little and cook for 4 Mins. more, until carrots are barely tender.

4. Pour carrots into air fryer baking pan.

5. Stir the honey mixture to combine well, pour glaze over carrots, and stir to coat.

6. Cook at 360°F for 1 minute or just until heated through.

Cheesy Potato Pot

 Servings: 4    **Cooking Time: 13 Mins.**

Ingredients:

- 3 C. cubed red potatoes (unpeeled, cut into ½-inch cubes)
- ½ tsp. garlic powder
- salt and pepper
- 1 tbsp. oil
- chopped chives for garnish (optional)
- Sauce
- 2 tbsp. milk
- 1 tbsp. butter
- 2 oz. sharp Cheddar cheese, grated
- 1 tbsp. sour cream

Directions:

1. Place potato cubes in large bowl and sprinkle with garlic, salt, and pepper. Add oil and stir to coat well.

2. Cook at 390°F for 13 Mins. or until potatoes are tender. Stir every 4 or 5minutes during cooking time.

3. While potatoes are cooking, combine milk and butter in a small saucepan. Warm over medium-low heat to melt butter. Add cheese and stir until it melts. The melted cheese will remain separated from the milk mixture. Remove from heat until potatoes are done.

4. When ready to serve, add sour cream to cheese mixture and stir over medium-low heat just until warmed. Place cooked potatoes in serving bowl. Pour sauce over potatoes and stir to combine.

5. Garnish with chives if desired.

Crispy Noodle Salad

Servings: 3   **Cooking Time: 22 Mins.**

Ingredients:

- 6 oz. Fresh Chinese-style stir-fry or lo mein wheat noodles
- 1½ tbsp. Cornstarch
- ¾ C. Chopped stemmed and cored red bell pepper
- 2 Medium scallion(s), trimmed and thinly sliced
- 2 tsp. Sambal oelek or other pulpy hot red pepper sauce (see here)
- 2 tsp. Thai sweet chili sauce or red ketchup-like chili sauce, such as Heinz
- 2 tsp. Regular or low-sodium soy sauce or tamari sauce
- 2 tsp. Unseasoned rice vinegar (see here)
- 1 tbsp. White or black sesame seeds

Directions:

1. Bring a large saucepan of water to a boil over high heat. Add the noodles and boil for 2 minutes. Drain in a colander set in the sink. Rinse several times with cold water, shaking the colander to drain the noodles very well. Spread the noodles out on a large cutting board and air-dry for 10 minutes.

2. Preheat the air fryer to 400°F.

3. Toss the noodles in a bowl with the cornstarch until well coated. Spread them out across the entire basket (although they will be touching and overlapping a bit). Air-fry for 6 minutes, then turn the solid mass of noodles over as one piece. If it cracks in half or smaller pieces, just fit these back together after turning. Continue air-frying for 6 minutes, or until golden brown and crisp.

4. As the noodles cook, stir the bell pepper, scallion(s), sambal oelek, red chili sauce, soy sauce, vinegar, and sesame seeds in a serving bowl until well combined.

5. Turn the basket of noodles out onto a cutting board and cool for a minute or two. Break the mass of noodles into individual noodles and/or small chunks and add to the dressing in the serving bowl. Toss well to serve.

Steak Fries

 **Servings: 4**   **Cooking Time: 20 Mins.**

Ingredients:

- 2 russet potatoes, scrubbed and cut into wedges lengthwise
- 1 tbsp. olive oil
- 2 tsp. seasoning salt (recipe below)

Directions:

1. Preheat the air fryer to 400°F.
2. Toss the potatoes with the olive oil and the seasoning salt.
3. Air-fry for 20 Mins. (depending on the size of the wedges), turning the potatoes over gently a few times throughout the cooking process to brown and cook them evenly.

Curried Fruit

 Servings: 6   **Cooking Time: 20 Mins.**

Ingredients:

- 1 C. cubed fresh pineapple
- 1 C. cubed fresh pear (firm, not overly ripe)
- 8 oz. frozen peaches, thawed
- 1 15-ounce can dark, sweet, pitted cherries with juice
- 2 tbsp. brown sugar
- 1 tsp. curry powder

Directions:

1. Combine all ingredients in large bowl. Stir gently to mix in the sugar and curry.
2. Pour into air fryer baking pan and cook at 360°F for 10minutes.
3. Stir fruit and cook 10 more minutes.
4. Serve hot.

Printed in Great Britain
by Amazon

21271096R00059